The GOODIES Rule OK

The GOODIES Rule OK

With contributions from
**Graeme Garden,
Bill Oddie
and Tim Brooke-Taylor**

ROBERT ROSS

CARLTON
BOOKS

Many thanks to:

Robin Clark, IBM, High Wycombe.

Lorna Russell, Carlton Books, West London.

Erin O'Neill, BBC Written Archives, Caversham.

Alan Coles, Henry Holland and Alan Parker for moral support.

Laura Beaumont for getting dusty in the name of picture research.

Jim Franklin and Bob Spiers for pointing me in the right direction.

Richard Jeffrey, BBC Picture Library, White City.

Bill Oddie, Tim Brooke-Taylor and Graeme Garden, The Goodies, Cricklewood.

First published in the UK by Carlton Books Ltd

20 Mortimer Street

London W1T 3JW

Text Copyright © Robert Ross 2006

Design Copyright © Carlton Books Ltd 2006

10-digit ISBN 1-84442-152-X

13-digit ISBN 978-1-84442-152-7

Editorial Manager: Lorna Russell

Picture Research: Paul Langan

Senior Art Editor: Emma Wicks

Designer: Simon Wilder

Production: Caroline Alberti

Printed in Dubai

The publishers would like to thank the following sources for their kind permission to reproduce the pictures in this book.

Key: t=Top, b=Bottom, c=Centre, l=Left, r=Right

BBC Photo Library: front flap, 2, 4, 10, 12-13, 16-17, 19, 25, 27, 28, 29, 30, 33, 34, 35l, 35r, 36-7, 38, 39, 44, 46, 47, 48bl, 48br, 48-49, 49, 53tr, 54, 54-55, 59, 60-61, 62, 63, 64-65, 66-67, 68, 68-69, 70, 72l, 72r, 76l, 76r, 77, 78t, 78b, 87bl, 87r, 89t, 89b, 90, 91tr, 91b, 92, 93l, 93r, 94, 96, 98, 99, 100l, 100r, 101, 102, 103, 104-105, 106tr, 106bl, 111, 116t, 116b, 117l, 117r, 118, 122, 123, 125, 126, 127, 128, 126, 130, 131, 134, 135, 136, 137, 139, 142-3, 144, 146, 148, 150, 151, 153, 156, 159, 161r, 162b, 162-3, 164, 164-5, 165, 166tr, 166bl, 184, 185br, back flap. **Big Laugh Comedy Attractions:** 180. **Corbis:** /Hulton-Deutsch Collection: 82 bl. **Private Collection:** 8, 11, 14l, 14r, 15, 17, 18, 20, 23, 24, 26, 28, 32, 40, 43t, 43l, 43r, 51, 52t, 52b, 53tl, 57l, 57r, 65t, 65b, 73tr, 73bl, 73br, 74t, 74b, 75tl, 75tr, 75br, 80, 82tl, 82tr, 84, 85, 88, 95l, 95r, 107, 108, 108-109, 109, 110c, 114, 119, 121, 124, 132-3, 140, 141, 147, 152, 155l, 155r, 158, 160l, 160r, 161l, 167, 170, 171t, 171b, 172, 175tl, 175bl, 175r, 178l, 178r, 179, 182, 183, 185tl, 186, 187, 188, 191, 192. **Redferns:** /BBC Photo Library: 112bl, 112-113 **Rex Features:** 174l; /Andre Csillag: 115; /London Weekend Television: 168, 173, 174, 176, 177

Every effort has been made to acknowledge correctly and contact the source and/or copyright holder of each picture and Carlton Books Limited apologises for any unintentional errors or omissions which will be corrected in future editions of this book.

CONTENTS

INTRODUCTION

The Goodies was a phenomenon. Between the end of 1970 and the start of 1982, the triumvirate consisting of writer-performers Tim Brooke-Taylor, Graeme Garden and Bill Oddie delivered some of the most imaginative television ever produced. Iconic images, including their unique mode of transport – the trandem – the giant kitten terrorising central London and the huge Dougal destroying the prime minister's country home, Chequers, remain indelible. A three-man team thinking as one, the shows combined relentlessly corny jokes with pioneering visual humour: 'Buster Keaton meets Tom and Jerry,' as Bill perceives it.

And, indeed, it was slapstick comedy and classic animation that inspired them. Talking at the peak of their fame, Tim mused: 'Ideally The Goodies will be great in seventy years time.' Halfway to that goal of longevity, the comedy still stands up remarkably well.

But, strangely, it has been over twenty years since the team has been regularly seen on British terrestrial television. Endlessly repeated during the show's long lifetime, there has been an almost conspiratorial refusal to repeat the programme since it came to an end. It is a situation that bemuses and bewilders the team. 'We were at the top of the tree for a decade,' points out Bill, 'and not only that, but we had five top-ten hit singles, the bestselling book for three consecutive years. No other show could boast of that.'

Unfairly stuck in a 1970s time warp of flared trousers and outrageous sideburns, *The Goodies* is a misunderstood comic treasure. This book marks the return of the Goodies.

Including material from the official BBC files and with exclusive memories from the Goodies themselves, this is the definitive record of what made the team what they were: one of the most thought-provoking and just plain hilarious comedy groups of all time.

I Sit In My Bath And I Have A Good Laugh

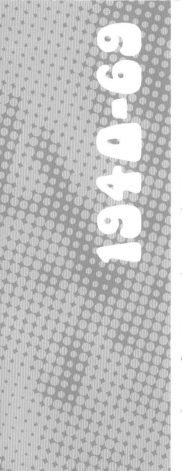

WAR BABIES

The Goodies was a product of Cambridge, or, more precisely, the celebrated Footlights of Cambridge University. For it was to that frivolous centre of that prestigious bastion of learning that three chaps from the North of England went in seek of knowledge, fun and the legacy of Peter Cook.

The first to be attracted was Timothy Julian Brooke-Taylor. Born on 17 July 1940 in Buxton, Derbyshire, his mother had been an international lacrosse player and taught at Cheltenham School, while her father, Parson Pawson, had played centre forward for England at the end of the nineteenth century.

But it was comedy that enraptured the young Tim; wireless heroes like Tony Hancock or Kenneth Horne, Sam Costa and Richard Murdoch: 'Much-Binding-in-the-Marsh was wonderful,' he recalls. 'I vividly remember at the end of the show them singing the signature tune. My heart would sink

Cos The Sig Tune Is Named After Me…

when they got to the last verse, it meant so much to me.' And film favourites like Abbott and Costello, 'especially when they met the monsters like the mummy or something. That wonderful mixture of giggling in a frightened way and laughing genuinely.' Trips to the pantomime, he says, 'left me in a state of sheer delight. I remember seeing the legendary Norman Evans as Dame in Manchester and Patrick Cargill. He was our local hero and part of the Buxton repertory company. He used to come round to our house and listen to our gramophone records. He wrote the pantos. He was so innovative. He would play Buttons on roller skates!'

By the age of twelve Tim's talent to amuse had won him attention. 'I was invited to a girl's birthday party purely because I made her mother laugh. I suppose that was a sort of compliment!'

Boarding at Winchester College, Tim was upset to discover that 'it had a very old-fashioned attitude towards acting. It was frowned upon because it was thought to encourage boys to show off! There were no school plays but the house I was in had impromptu revues at the end of each term. As a new boy I was expected to perform something for my house on the last night of term. I was terrified and felt it was extremely cruel to put the youngest boy under so much pressure. However I decided to do a bit of conjuring. I had a few tricks up my sleeve, amongst other places.

The first trick was a disaster. "The card you have in your hand is an ace of spades." It was a jack of hearts. The red handkerchief turned into a . . . red handkerchief. By now there were suppressed giggles. Something told me to make it look as if all the tricks were going wrong on purpose. It worked, and the suppressed giggles were turned into joyful howls of approval. I did many sketches after this, only to forty boys or so, but it led to a report from my housemaster who said, "if all else fails he could become a film star or, as he'd probably prefer, a music-hall comedian".'

However, Tim chose to study law. 'All my family were lawyers. We were part of a Derbyshire enlarged family with solicitors in Buxton, Bakewell and Matlock. I was going to join my elder brother Martin in our father's old office in Buxton. The firm is still called Brooke-Taylors.' But in order to study at Cambridge Tim had to convince the Derbyshire Education Committee.

'My father had died and there wasn't any money so I was literally begging for a grant. I remember the committee asking me, "What are you going to do besides work the whole time?" I was a little taken aback because,

'Talented Timbo' in a rather dashing early Goodies portrait.

quite frankly, I wasn't expecting to work *all* the time! The Footlights came to me. I had no intention of doing anything like this. I wasn't prepared for this question. I knew the correct answer – that I'd be drinking and generally enjoying myself – would not get any grant! I recalled my brother talking about the Footlights and was panicked into mentioning them. I wouldn't have had the nerve to join if I hadn't promised the grant committee! In fact, it was so important to me that I had several sleepless nights before my Footlights audition.'

'And,' recalls Tim, 'I became a fan of Peter Cook during my first year. I bought eight tickets for the opening night of *Beyond the Fringe* and eight for the last night. I'd heard great things and assumed I could sell these on. I had huge difficulty passing them on for the first night, but there was a queue for the last night. *Beyond the Fringe* is still funnier than anything else I've seen. I remember banging my head on the seat in front of me because I was laughing so much. I benefited from Peter being in the same college as myself because, although he had left the university the term before I arrived, he left behind a great reputation for the Pembroke College Smoking

Musical director Hugh Macdonald, Tim and Tony Buffery put together *A Clump of Plinths*.

Concert. Much of the material for this event ended up in the West End even when he was still an undergraduate. The Pembroke Smoker, as it was called, was where I, Bill, Jonathan Lynn and Eric Idle all started our Cambridge comedy capers.'

However, Tim's first encounter with Cambridge dramatics wasn't a success. 'When I got to Cambridge I attended the Societies' Fair and found the Footlights people too clever and too grand. The answer, I thought, was to aim lower and audition for a college play. I auditioned for a part in a Pembroke College production of Sheridan's *The Critics*. Thirty-three people auditioned for the play including myself. There were thirty-two parts. I didn't get one! Eventually I was taken on, when someone fell ill, as the "Left Bank of the Thames".'

For his first year, 1960–1, Tim read Economics and Politics, largely to avoid the arduous task of Roman Law, but found himself spending most of his time with John Cleese and Graham Chapman. 'John was a bit of a swot actually. I mean he used to go to all the law lectures! But we were good friends. We would revise together. He generously lent me his lecture notes and, of course, in exam situations, B for Brooke-Taylor and C for Cleese were sat near each other. One of the points he had anticipated came up as the very first question so I was able to turn round and signal, "Thank you very much, John!"'

But it was comedy that brought Tim and Bill Oddie together. 'Poppy Day was the big charity day in Cambridge,' recalls Tim. 'One or two of us did some sketches for a very amateur charity show. One of them was Bill. I was very impressed. He was an exhibitioner, had played cricket for Warwickshire schools and was a pretty useful rugby player. At least, that's what he said. He had a bit of a chip on the shoulder about public schoolboys and this

A quartet that changed the face of British comedy. Jonathan Miller, Alan Bennett, Dudley Moore and Peter Cook in *Beyond the Fringe*.

Tim and Tony Buffery run through their latest skit.

Bill promoting his 1965 disc 'The Knitting Song'.

prejudice took a lot of overcoming. It was ironical really as his school, King Edward VI, Birmingham, was one of the best in the country. I was particularly impressed with his musical ability and even then he was producing brilliant musical parodies.'

William Edgar Oddie had been born on 7 July 1941 in Rochdale, Lancashire. At King Edward VI's he had met Nat Joseph, the composer of a musical school review, in which he cast Bill. 'I have no idea why he did this!' says Bill. 'I had absolutely no show business connection whatsoever. And I had absolutely no confidence in myself. That first one started a sort of tradition and I was in the second one the following year. It was always the musical side that I was involved in. I even remember making up silly lyrics for the school rugby songs, so that's as far back as I can trace any songwriting leanings.'

By the time he attended Pembroke College, to read English, his natural ear for music had fully matured although, at first, he found Cambridge 'a rather frightening

place. It was a strange time. Some of them were much older than me and had even done National Service. Others had so many connections in London show business that they were treating Cambridge as almost an irritating interruption to their careers. It was only down to John Cleese and Tim that I got "in" to the Footlights circle. I was the only one at that time writing contemporary-sounding music; funny songs with a rock'n'roll or pop feel. Up to that point everything had been a bit twee. Almost everybody did a "funny" Gilbert and Sullivan number for their audition!'

Tim's audition had proved inspired. 'Peter Cook had done these incredible shows for his three years at Pembroke,' he recalls. 'I did a piece from that for my audition for the Footlights.'

The year was 1962 and Tim was made the junior treasurer and sat on the script committee for the revue of that year, *Double Take*. John Cleese, who had already contributed material to the previous year's effort, *I*

Thought I Saw It Move, was the committee's Registrar, and Graham Chapman was the Member Without Portfolio. Bill was credited with writing additional material.

Double Take was a fairly inauspicious start. Robert Atkins, the president of the Footlights, was outraged over producer Trevor Nunn's production of *Much Ado About Nothing*: 'He was doing something for the Marlowe Society,' remembers Tim, 'and he took half our budget!' As a result, 'the set was this wrought-iron monstrosity on which none of us felt very comfortable'. The company featured Tim alongside Chapman, Cleese, Atkins, Miriam Margolyes, Humphrey Barclay, Nigel Brown, Tony Hendra and Alan George. 'Some of the material was very good and we used it again later on radio and television, but we all felt it lacked any real energy,' confides Tim. 'It was also a complete rejection of the satire movement that had made the Footlights' name. Robert Atkins, like me, had a sense of music-hall tradition, which was fun, but some of it was so embarrassing it made my toes curl. It still does. John, Graham and myself would lumber on stage in skins and start singing, "We're a most important caveman!" It had the most dreadful dance routines imaginable. Truly awful. I still get a cold sweat when I think about it! Suffice to say the Pythons didn't recreate that at the Hollywood Bowl!'

'And I didn't write it either!' insists Bill. 'I wrote one song for

Double Take inspired by a story I had read about Adam Faith having had an audience with the Archbishop of Canterbury! I know it sounds bizarre, but it was a big story at the time. It made all the papers! It was a break from the usual and it went down very well with the audience. I think, even as late as then, rock'n'roll still had a slightly naughty reputation. It was certainly more raucous than the stuff they were used to and it got a lot of laughs.'

As a result, Bill also got his first taste of television success. 'Television was my first proper job after leaving Cambridge,' he reflects. 'Actually I was still at Cambridge when I got my first job. People were in the habit of coming up from the BBC and watching the Footlights shows and occasionally buying some material for television. I had written this song for the revue and it was subsequently bought for *That Was The Week That Was*. So that's how it all started!'

Although the company took *Double Take* to the Edinburgh fringe, 1962 was, more importantly, the year that Tim and Bill met Graeme.

David Graeme Garden was born on 18 February 1943 in Aberdeen, Scotland, moving to Preston, Lancashire in 1947. 'When I was nine I was ever so good at falling over!' he smiles. 'In fact, I used

Bill the disgruntled Goody in 1980.

**Above: Tim and John Cleese on the brink of comic immortality.
Left: David Frost's groundbreaking *TW3* with Roy Kinnear,
Kenneth Cope, Lance Percival and Willie Rushton.**

to be invited to perform before the assembled company.
Mainly my family, school friends and their families!'

Educated at Repton School, Graeme enjoyed drama
but his real passion was for art, discovering he possessed
a talent as a cartoonist. But it was medicine that took
him to Cambridge, studying at Emmanuel College from
1961. Still, he sated his love of performance by joining
the Cambridge University Light Entertainment Society
(C.U.L.E.S.). Naturally, his friendship with fellow medical
student Graham Chapman would lead him to the Footlights.
'You could turn up and pretty much do whatever you
wanted to do at the Smokers. I was auditioned by Tim! I'd
seen some of the Footlights shows and thought, "I'm not
going to take them on at their own game." I did a quick
sketch which got me in!'

'Graeme was excellent,' says Tim, 'but he really just
went through the motions of auditioning. I knew his work
from the C.U.L.E.S. and had appeared in one of their
shows with him. He did a very good drawing routine, a bit
like a superior Rolf Harris. His "Pet's Corner" routine was
proving a big hit even at this stage.'

'And,' adds Bill with a smile, 'he's been doing it ever
since. I suppose "Kitten Kong" is the best showcase but,
even today, give Graeme a bit of rag and some fluff and he

Cambridge Circus rehearsed for the New Zealand tour in the ballroom of Crathorne Hall. The team's drummer, Jamie Dugdale, was the son of Lord and Lady Crathorne who are joined by John Cleese, Graham Chapman, Tim, David Hatch, Humphrey Barclay (saluting) and (in bowler hats) Jean Hart, Jo Kendall and Anne Hatch.

will create life for you on the spot!'

Tim reflects: 'that same year I also auditioned and accepted Eric Idle, so as a talent scout I think I've proved to be rather good. I also gave Humphrey Barclay his first job as a director. Perhaps I should have been an agent!'

That was a career move never considered thanks almost entirely to the 1963 Footlights revue. The year saw Tim become president, with John Cleese and Graeme Garden sitting on the committee. The show was called *A Clump of Plinths*. 'We got that title after a recount that Humphrey Barclay had fiddled,' says Tim. 'The title most people wanted was *You Can't Call A Show "Cornflakes"*, which I suppose is a better one!'

Again the company endured a minimalist set, dominated by huge cardboard boxes that could be used and rearranged as each item dictated. John Cleese and Bill scripted a Somerset Maugham parody that created the characters of stuffy romantics John and Mary. As played by Cleese and Jo Kendall, these characters were later resurrected for radio's *I'm Sorry I'll Read That Again*. Bill also composed 'Green Line Bus', a song that saw bowler-hatted London businessmen discussing bus routes in the style of a Negro spiritual. Tim excelled in 'Swap-a-Jest', a two-hander with Chris Stuart-Clark that saw an Elizabethan discourse in the style of a music-hall double act. 'I wrote quite a bit at this stage,' says Tim, 'usually with Chris. And quite a bit with Bill, John Cleese and Graham Chapman.' And, although not in the company, Graeme contributed some written material.

The revue proved so popular that impresario Michael White suggested they bypass the Edinburgh fringe entirely. 'He was a great impresario, was Michael,' reflects Bill, 'He had got this reputation for taking risks, and, boy, did he take a risk with us.'

The 'professorial' Graeme. The firm's brain-box.

Equipped with Equity cards, the company played a one-week engagement at the Robin Hood theatre, Averham, and a further week at the York Festival. The *Observer* singled out Bill, venturing that he was 'probably born a professional comic. The sooner he reaches London the better.' And, on 10 July 1963, the show, retitled *Cambridge Circus*, did indeed open at the New Arts Theatre.

'The satire boom was still very powerful on television,' says Tim, 'but we all felt that *Beyond the Fringe* had taken that as far as it could be taken. I suppose our show was just silly and audiences seemed to love it!' Indeed, the original three-week run was extended to five due to popular demand.

By common consent, the show stopper was John Cleese's 'Judge Not' sketch. 'John seemed to have been writing that sketch for as long as anyone could remember,' says Bill. 'It was always "almost" ready but never was. Finally he presented this sketch and it was hilarious!'

For Tim it was particularly enjoyable. 'There had been a lot of lawyers in my family so it was sort of expected I would follow suit . . . and I liked law a lot. It's funny, a lot of lawyers do comedy, simply because there is so much scope. The cases we used to study used to have me in hysterics because they were so sick! I used to start giggling when we were told about this case when a runaway coach and horses turned a corner, and frightened a pregnant woman who then gave birth to an idiot child. Or a little old lady who was literally locked in a lavatory and tried to climb out. She put one foot on the toilet bowl, the other on the toilet roll! By this stage I had lost all control. Who wouldn't? John and I used to love all that and that certainly informed his "Judge Not" sketch, which I think was the best sketch we did in the revue.'

Importantly, it was an item that never seemed to be played the same twice. 'It was a basic structure that John had written but we used to do all sorts of mad things with it,' explains Tim. 'I played this company director cum music-hall comic called Sidney Molar. Now he was totally ad-libbed one night and stayed. That company was so good. We could pretty much get away with doing anything, we all knew each other so well. I also played an ancient courtroom employee who went out of control somewhat.'

The radio arts programme, *The Critics*, singled out Tim's decrepit performance as a 'masterly parody of Jean Martin's Lucky in the original French production of *Waiting For Godot*.' 'Of course it was!' grins Tim.

'And he milked it for all it was worth,' confirms Bill. 'He had to bring on this bidet as Exhibit A and he made this character older and older and older as the run went on. He would take a minute to get on stage, another minute to get the exhibit in place and another minute to get off! Eventually, just as he was getting off, one of us would shout, "Hold on . . . come back here!" and he would have to turn round and take another minute to get on again!'

Bill was, according to the *Guardian*, a 'real discovery; a slightly more dazed version of the young Mickey Rooney, a dazzling comic who should go far'. 'I'd nominate for stardom 21-year-old Bill Oddie, who wrote many of the numbers and sings them, too,' said the *Evening News*. The *Star* celebrated 'a small, square, india-rubber figure like a highly muscular baby, who sings, dances and fools with huge bounce and minute precision'.

The show transferred to the Lyric on 14 August 1963, although original cast member Anthony W.H. Buffery, not expecting this sort of success, dropped out, allowing Graham Chapman to take his place. By the end of the run on 9 November 1963, *Cambridge Circus* had played over a hundred performances. Before the final curtain Chris Stuart-Clark bowed out to be replaced by original producer Humphrey Barclay. It was with this cast that the BBC recorded a half-hour highlights programme for broadcast at the end of December 1963.

The show proved popular enough for the BBC to record and broadcast three further programmes throughout April 1964. Initially retitled *Get Off My Foot*, these programmes were eventually broadcast as *I'm Sorry I'll Read That Again*. 'It was what every announcer said on the BBC if he made a mistake,' remembers Tim, 'and it always made John and I laugh!' Moreover, Michael White had set up a six-week tour of New Zealand from May 1964.

Billed as 'Masters of Mirth', the team (now joined by Jonathan Lynn) played to enthused audiences with Bill, apparently, 'equipped with roller-bearings for feet and an iron-plated voice that can handle "pop" songs. He is irresistible whether gyrating wildly as an Asian rock'n'roll singer, hanging by his fingertips as a dwarf witness or suffering silently as a pie-throwing demonstrator,' according to the New Zealand *Herald*. During the tour the team also recorded four more radio programmes for the New Zealand market.

Graeme, meanwhile, was still studying. He had also been appointed president of the Footlights for 1964 and was writing and appearing in the revue, *Stuff What Dreams Are Made Of*, with David Gooderson and Guy Slater. He remembers: 'During my presidency there was a strong

Brits on Broadway ... although the experience was a mixed one.

movement for women to be admitted to the Footlights as full members. The late great Harry Porter, senior treasurer and later archivist, was very set in his ways, and threatened to resign if women were admitted. I think he knew it would be inevitable, and was making a last stand, but the result was, in spite of my efforts, women were not admitted that year. After that, under Eric Idle's presidency they were welcomed in. The review that year had a cast that included Jonathan Lynn (now a Hollywood director) and John Cameron (who went on to compose the scores for many movies). I probably did "Pet's Corner", and we had a Beatles number led by Cameron, which was lent to the chaps on tour in the USA, as they thought the Americans would understand it.'

Broadway producer Sol Hurok, noted for his presentations

of ballet and opera, booked *Cambridge Circus* for a run at the Plymouth Theatre, New York, from 6 October 1964. It ran for just 23 performances. 'That was thanks to Michael White again,' recalls Bill. 'He stayed in England but he had approached Hurok who said, "Sure, I'll put these guys on!" I'm convinced to this day that it was a huge tax dodge just like *The Producers*, or if that wasn't the case, it was just that Hurok seemingly had no idea what he was taking on. We were called *Cambridge Circus* because of where we had originated from and because of where we had played in London, and I think he saw that title and thought he would be getting a spectacular three-ring circus from England . . . with real British lions! He would come in and say, "Where are the elephants?"'

'I didn't really enjoy that experience,' says Tim, 'although it was amazing to be in New York! Everything had happened so fast, we were almost blasé about going to America. Then we were very cross when they wanted to start cutting sketches. An Oscar Wilde piece, with me as Dame Edith Evans, went for starters!' However, Eric Idle, still at Cambridge, had sent over a timely Hallelujah chorus in the style of the Beatles, which had featured in *Stuff What Dreams Are Made Of*. 'We literally had to perform it the next day, so there was no time to rehearse,' remembers Tim. 'My only contribution was to suggest we play the mop-tops like choirboys so that we could have hymn books in our hands. That was to stop our hands shaking from fear! But we got an encore for it. We never did it again. We didn't dare!'

But it was another item, 'Humour Without Tears', which caught the public imagination. Added to the show in New Zealand, it had been written by Oxford students Terry Jones and Michael Palin. A memorable masterclass in slapstick comedy technique, it was performed by Tim, Bill and Jonathan Lynn, with David Hatch intoning the deadpan lecture. The reviewers were impressed, none more so than Walter Kerr of the all-powerful New York *Herald Tribune*. On Saturday 24 October 1964, the Sunday papers were delivered early and, as the company performed on Broadway for the final time, Kerr's piece celebrated them as comedy greats. 'Humour Without Tears', in particular, was picked out because: 'having been told that something is hilarious we are shown that it is just plain unbearable, thank you, and as a result it becomes hilarious. That is a very nice parlay, and I couldn't be more admiring.'

Bill reflects that 'I would actually get the best notices, purely because I was doing the music as well – the critics recognised the concept of songs and praised me accordingly! They could easily compartmentalise.' Indeed, the *Journal American* commented: 'It appears that Mr Oddie, aside from appearing in most of the sketches with great success, has also written many of them and also much of the music, which is highly acceptable if not immortal.' Perceptively, the New York *Daily News* pondered: 'Bill Oddie may be the outsider in the bunch, though. He is small, a stylish, funny dancer and he can sing as fast as Danny Kaye.'

'So I got rave reviews in America and London,' says Bill. 'Tim was probably next and John Cleese was nowhere. We always thought John was the funny one, which just shows that writer-performers know far more than critics do. Or indeed audiences. It was obvious to us that John was the genius. He was the original. We could have told people that years before he was "discovered". We could also have told them how crap I was! I just jumped around and sang a bit!'

But all the critical praise counted for little when the cast had to face the fact that 'nobody was coming to see the show. The audiences were very poor,' says Bill. 'We would go in to a ticket agency and say, "How's it going with *Cambridge Circus*?" and they would look dumbly at us and say, "I'm sorry? Cambridge what? I don't appear to have that here!" They literally weren't selling tickets for it. I think Hurok thought, "Oh, shit. What have I done? I better run this into the ground and get these guys off Broadway as quickly as possible."'

However, such was the media interest in the show in America that Bill had the opportunity to jump around and sing a bit on *The Ed Sullivan Show*. 'We did all the chat shows,' reflects Bill, 'but Sullivan was *the* show to be on. We were on with The Animals. I got mistaken for Eric Burdon and got all his cast off! It was lovely that was! Although he didn't get much, really. He had terrible skin!' The team also found themselves performing at the JFK Library in Connecticut and a small theatre in Greenwich Village, New York, where they played until February 1965. 'That was after just three weeks on Broadway,' says Bill. 'The venue was the Second City Club, which was a very famous improvisation group. We were there for about nine months and, of course, it was a venue far more suited to what we were doing, but the notices just vanished once we left Broadway itself.'

At this stage an entirely American cast took over, with Tim retained to oversee rehearsals and initial performances. 'It was awful,' he remembers. 'Here were great American performers who were very funny, but the director was insisting on them copying what we had done. Even down to silly nervous tics. They couldn't hope to duplicate what we had done. We had written it and lived it for months. These poor people were thrown in at the deep end and sank rather quickly.'

After *Cambridge Circus* closed, several of the cast stayed in America. John Cleese opened in *Half a Sixpence* on Broadway while Tim and Bill appeared in a touring production of David Frost's *That Was The Week That Was*. 'I was a contract writer and sometimes performer on the television show,' remembers Bill. 'That was my main job and I was paid to write a song and two or three minutes of material every week. When we came back to London after something like two years doing the show in the theatre I got an agent who didn't really know what to do with me.'

In fact, Diana Crawfurd of Noel Gay Artists Limited, wrote to Frank Muir in December 1964 promoting Bill:

. . . as the author of several of the funniest sketches in TW3 and of some of Millie's [Millicent Martin's] jazzers, and also of 'BBCBCTV' in David Frost's Degree of Frost. He is due to return from America early in the New Year and would be available for anything in which you thought he might be suitable. In any event, I would love him to have a talk with you as he may well be able to write himself one of your 45-minute specials. Again, maybe you would have something in Comedy Playhouse, for which he would be right.

Bill remembers, 'I was saying "I'd like to do a bit of everything," but they were saying, "No, you can't do that, you have to specialise," so I said, "Well, OK, I suppose I'm a writer." And that was that. There was *That Was The Week That Was*, but I was also farmed out to other programmes. I wrote for Ronnie Barker, and Hope and Keen, and Tommy Cooper. Writing for Tommy was the most completely pointless exercise of all because he wouldn't remember a bloody word you wrote! You knew he was funny. Inevitably he was funny. He was someone like Frankie Howerd who could be funny forgetting the script and bumbling his way through it. You would give him the sketch and he'd say, "What's this? I don't understand this! Oh, I've dropped it on the floor . . . oh dear . . ." It was the most depressing thing to do, because you knew that your stuff would never be heard! I also did a special song for Lulu and Alan Price which I was rather proud of. But *TW3* was hailed as something amazing. And it was important. It simply allowed you to make jokes about a wider range of subjects. A wider range of people. The jokes weren't new. It was just instead of saying, "I say, I say, I say . . . my mother-in-law . . ." you could say, "I say, I say, I say . . . Harold Macmillan!"'

Tim remembers the live version as 'great fun. David Frost wasn't in it really, of course, but he would turn up sometimes and make an appearance. He kept telling the

A thing for ferrets! The classic *ISIRTA* line-up of Tim, David Hatch, Jo Kendall, John Cleese, Bill and Graeme.

announcer that "I'm the star of this you know . . . don't forget!" And, of course, he was the star. It was his show. And the audiences were great. We would play to three hundred people in intimate revue and the next night it would be a stadium-sized audience of six thousand! We had fashioned it for an American audience but they seemed to enjoy the more obvious English humour.'

It was radio that brought Tim, Graeme and Bill together for the first time professionally. Having noticed that the fledgling *I'm Sorry I'll Read That Again* programmes had proved successful, the BBC commissioned a series. Tim and Bill were available, as were David Hatch and Jo Kendall. John Cleese was still in America and Graham Chapman had decided to return to his medical studies. Another funny doctor was drafted in to replace him – Graeme Garden.

On 28 May 1965 the team recorded the first episode of the series. Initially the show consisted of vintage sketches from Cambridge revues and, as a result, the performers shared a writing credit. Cleese joined the fun for series two but by the third, broadcast from October 1966, Graeme found his medical training getting in the way. He had to opt out of performing in favour of a midwifery course in Plymouth, although he regularly contributed to the scripts by scribbling lines of dialogue on the back of envelopes and posting them to producer Humphrey Barclay.

Although the radio series continued to go from strength to strength and attract a very vocal cult following, the team sensed an atmosphere at Broadcasting House. 'It was getting to the stage that when I asked for the simplest thing it was like I was asking for the earth,' says Bill. 'The executives would look at us and say, "There once was a programme called *The Goon Show* and they don't work for us any more, so don't get uppity with us!" We all thought, yes, and look at them, making a fortune on television and in films! What sort of argument is that!'

For Tim, it was television that held the most interest. On 21 May 1965 BBC producer Peter Titheradge wrote to Frank Muir:

Would you see a chap for me and have a perfectly general talk with him about television prospects in the BBC in some sort of production capacity. Chap's name is Tim Brooke-Taylor and he was the 1962/63 President of the Cambridge Footlights. This was the ultra-successful year that produced Cambridge Circus . . . Tim was a leading light throughout (he is a very good comic) as well as contributing material – mainly in the form of ideas, I understand. He has now just arrived back in this country and is looking for fresh fields to conquer!

The mercurial Spike Milligan making an entrance on Tim's *This Is Your Life* in 1981.

In July of that year, Tim secured a meeting with Tom Sloan at the BBC with a view to signing up for the General Production Course. Alas, Sloan discovered that there were no vacancies and suggested meeting again in the autumn. Tim, writing on 29 July 1965, was:

> . . . naturally, extremely disappointed . . . *[however] I should like, if I may, to take you up on your kind offer to come and see you again in the near future, as our discussion the other day was extremely valuable to me. It is very difficult to have any firm ideas or make any decisions in a vacuum, and you managed to clarify the situation considerably which makes things much easier. Since seeing you the other day I have been doing a great deal of rethinking and have become absolutely certain, in my own mind, that what I want to do is work in Television Comedy in some capacity, and from my own limited experience, for the BBC.*

However, Tim revealed, 'I have been asked by ATV to join the [Bernard] Braden production team for the new series, which would run through until next summer.'

The show was *On the Braden Beat* and Tim had been drafted in as a replacement for Peter Cook's celebrated E.L. Wisty character. He recalls, 'I was this right-wing, racist bigot and, ironically, became a hero to many people. I found people were beginning to agree with my obnoxious character. It was a bit like Alf Garnett in that respect. I even got censored! I was doing a piece about Princess Margaret, who had been naughty in the West Indies. I gave my advice as "she must remember at all times that she is British, at least on her mother's side". That was changed to "she must remember when she's in Mustique, she's not just abroad, she's a Princess!" Even that got complaints!'

Tim also wrote for Spike Milligan on the ATV sketch show *Milligan's Wake*. 'I learned very early on that Spike liked a beginning, a middle and an end to a sketch and room to move in-between. By that I mean he only felt comfortable with it when he could add his own slant. I wrote a piece about a peer who has fallen on hard times

A *TAF* roll call: Beverley, Jonathan Lynn, Ronald Fletcher, Dilys Watling, Graeme, Bill and Tony Buffery.

and lives in a council house. He shoots the plastic ducks off the wall. Spike took the basic idea and wrote in a butler who came out of a wardrobe and said, "Time for your heart attack, sir!" That was the genius of the man.'

Bill had also continued his television career, writing for *On the Braden Beat* as well as appearing as the folk singer Hooligan; a parody of Donovan. From October 1965 Bill was appearing in the satirical programme *BBC3*. 'That was no fun, really. Satire was dead and Ned Sherrin, who was producing it, just seemed interested in song and dance. There was more and more dancing and less and less satire as far as I was concerned!'

Still, it was *Twice A Fortnight* that pointed the way forward. It was produced and directed by Tony Palmer as a major vehicle for Graeme. Although still contributing to *I'm Sorry I'll Read That Again*, Graeme passed his medical

examinations in 1967 and had a job already lined up. It was flatmate Eric Idle who intervened by introducing Graeme to his agent, Roger Hancock. 'Roger was quite stern with me actually,' says Graeme. 'He said, "Look here, you can't just muck about, you know. If you want to write for a hobby, fine. But if you want to take it seriously people won't just phone up and offer you work. You have to go out there and find it!" You couldn't write this, but this is what happened. The moment he said that the phone rang and it was Tony Palmer saying, "I understand you represent Graeme Garden. Would he be interested in this television series I have for him!" That was it. I worked very hard for it as well!'

The scripts were written with Bill, Terry Jones and Michael Palin – 'And it was like a rock group in a way,' reflects Bill. 'We were interacting with the Oxford guys who

At last! John Cleese, Marty Feldman, Graham Chapman and Tim in the innovative *1948 Show*.

would go on to do *Python* and we also had old Cambridge guys like Tony Buffery and Jonathan Lynn in it as well.' But Bill locked horns with Palmer over the musical content. 'I naturally wanted to use my own stuff but Palmer, who was a brilliant man and made brilliant music documentaries later, just wouldn't see it my way. I was a scriptwriter and a performer. The music was somebody else's concern as far as Palmer was concerned. Mind you, he got some terrific guests on the show. The Who. The Small Faces. The Moody Blues.'

Graeme also found Palmer hard to fathom. 'He was known as "the *enfant terrible* of television directing" and that was perfect. He really was an "awful child". He would storm around the studio shouting, "I don't understand this! I don't understand any of this!" He thought if we were in a nervous panic we would be funnier. We just felt like having a nervous breakdown, frankly!'

Broadcast from October 1967, the show was important

inasmuch as it allowed Bill and Graeme to experiment with visual comedy. 'It was a very strange late-night show,' admits Bill. 'We actually used to subtitle it "Match of the Day (part 2)" to try and get someone to watch it! It was very late at night, not late enough some people thought, I'm sure. It really was a terrible mess, but I suppose you can see it as an important mess if you want to!'

However, the show certainly had its fans. A Miss C. Miller of Manchester wrote to the BBC on 19 January 1968:

It has come to my notice, after the showing of that most wonderful programme Twice A Fortnight, Bill Oddie should have his own television programme. These are not only my own feelings, but those of Mr. Bill Oddie himself who put me up to this. He wrote in his last letter to me, 'If you wrote simply to BBC TV Centre, Shepherds Bush, London demanding my reappearance I'm sure it would

Graeme as Mr. Billy the music hall comedian in
Twice A Fortnight.

*have great effect . . .' I know several people in
'the 'eart of the North' who would welcome such a
great star into their homes, and even the critics are
beginning to say how good Twice A Fortnight was
(RIP). Hoping you will take note of this letter.*

Now represented by David Conyers of ALS Management
Limited, three days before Miss Miller put pen to paper
Conyers bigged up his client to BBC bigwig Bill Cotton
Jnr. 'Bill has a number of ideas for musical programmes
which he would like to discuss with you and he would also
very much like to be considered as a writer and composer
for any forthcoming musical programmes you may have
scheduled.'

While Bill and Graeme were struggling to make a mark
with *Twice A Fortnight*, Tim was enjoying popularity in the
second series of a rather more ground-breaking sketch
show from David Frost. Having already contributed to
The Frost Report and *The Frost Programme*, *At Last the
1948 Show* was designed as a showcase for Tim Brooke-
Taylor and John Cleese. The two principals, however,
were convinced that the series needed a team. If Graham
Chapman was a natural choice, then Frost writer Marty

Feldman was an inspired one. 'I got to know Marty very
well,' says Tim. 'He was a brilliant writer but nobody
was using him as a performer. For John and I, this was
madness. For one thing he looked funny with that mad
stare, and for another he was a very talented performer.
As a writer he was tireless. He would be spending half
the week writing the radio series *Round the Horne* with
Barry Took and the rest of the week writing sketches for
television with me.' Chapman and Cleese would invariably
write together but 'sometimes the four of us would sit
down and throw ideas around', reflects Tim. 'That's how
the "Four Yorkshiremen" sketch was written.'

Feldman also helped Tim in performance. 'We were
rehearsing this sketch where John was the psychiatrist
and I was a patient with a pathological fear of rabbits!
John was going through the motions really, underplaying
everything, and I had nothing to react to. I got very
depressed because the whole sketch fell flat and so I went
over to Marty and said, "This isn't working, I've nothing
to be frightened of!" Marty, God love him, said, "On the
recording, wait thirty seconds and then stamp on his foot!"
It worked. John's look of absolute fury gave me the fear I
needed. John, professional at all times, went straight on
with the sketch, but the anger was still there!'

By the time *At Last the 1948 Show* came to an end
in November 1967, Feldman was already being lined
up for his own BBC show. *It's Marty* would become an
award-winning success and featured Tim as the principal
'second banana'. Broadcast between April 1968 and
January 1969, the show's initial popularity proved a
further springboard for Tim.

Broaden Your Mind: an Encyclopaedia of the Air, first hit
the screen in October 1968 and headlined Tim alongside
Graeme. 'I think the mistake there was to rely on old sketches
from our revues and radio shows,' admits Graeme. 'The
bits that were less successful were things which we hadn't
conceived for television. I suppose *Twice A Fortnight* had

Writing *Doctor in the House*. Series script editor Barry Cryer, novelist Richard Gordon and scribes Graham Chapman, Graeme, John Cleese and Bill.

given me an understanding of what worked on television. Simply transferring old stage routines to the studio didn't. All the comedy was in the dialogue. There was no character. No heart to the sketches.'

The heart came with two delightful old buffers called Sir Edward Windward and Professor Frederick Pottermore. Teddy and Freddy were played by Graeme and Tim respectively, and Tim believes that 'we fell in love with them. Perhaps too much. Graeme and I would be happy doing the Teddy and Freddy sketches all the time in any show. They were these dotty old friends who just rambled on about history or nature. It was lovely playing that.'

Although it was the first major television series to feature Tim, Graeme and Bill, Bill says, 'I don't remember doing much for the show.' Indeed, he made only one on-screen appearance – in episode four – and enjoyed a

writing credit for recycled Cambridge material. However, Bill was the natural choice as co-writer when Graeme landed a lucrative assignment with Thames television.

'*Doctor in the House* had, of course, been a huge success as a film in the fifties and that film series was still going, on and off,' says Graeme. 'The television series was totally different. The pilot was written by John Cleese and Dr Graham Chapman. However, they were at the same time developing *Python* and decided they couldn't write both series at once. Bill and I had been writing for *I'm Sorry I'll Read That Again* and John called me to ask if we would be interested in taking on the bulk of the writing for the *Doctor* series. I said yes, and off we went. Humphrey Barclay was pleased to have medical writers, me and Graham, on board and we did use our own experiences or apocryphal tales we'd heard at medical school, which

Broaden Your Mind with Graeme, Nick McArdle and Tim.

were quite different from the stories in Richard Gordon's wonderful books, simply because everyone already knew the gags about "What's the bleeding time?" and "Big breaths". And having been to medical school I did know which end was which of a stethoscope!'

Series two of *Broaden Your Mind* followed almost immediately. Bill rewrote such popular *I'm Sorry I'll Read That Again* songs as 'On Ilkley Moor Baht 'At', 'We Love Jimmy Young', 'One-Man Band', 'Hoogey Boogey Boo' and 'Walt Disney', to fit the television production numbers. He also contributed at least one original song, 'Football Choir', and was brought fully on board as a major player in the programme. 'I honestly thought a lot of the first series was very safe and cosy and nice,' says Bill. 'I like my comedy with a bit of bite. I'm all for annoying people if I can! It was actually Barry Cryer who contacted me. Tim and Graeme were getting too nice, really, so he said, "Come in and be unpleasant!" So I did!'

Graeme and Tim had also clearly got the message.

Teddy and Freddy were dropped from the series in favour of the 'Buffies'; three elderly residents of a gentlemen's club played by Graeme, Tim and *It's Marty* stalwart Roland MacLeod. Another new addition to the series was Graeme as the cold-hearted Dr Fiendish of the British Institute of Applied Science and Not Germ Warfare. 'He was a nasty piece of work,' chuckles Graeme. 'Certainly not the sort of person you would want to spend much time with. But we were told to be nastier, so we were!'

Tim was happy with the latest batch of *Broaden Your Mind*, which came to the end of its run on 29 December 1969. 'I remember the series going very well and everybody seemed happy with it,' reflects Tim. 'Then we got a note from Michael Mills saying something like, "Yes, that was good, but you won't be doing any more of those will you?" I actually thought we might at the time, but I suppose at the back of our minds *Broaden Your Mind* was a cover to hatch this idea for a series which became *The Goodies*.'

Take a Little Good Advice. Try a Trip to Paradise…

ANYTHING, ANYWHERE, ANYTIME

Although most of the material for the second series of *Broaden Your Mind* had been written by Graeme and Tim, Graeme maintains, 'I can write very quickly with someone – as long as that someone is Bill! We have very little in common apart from our senses of humour. Tim and I are too similar. We just sit around and natter about things and never get down to actually writing. I always needed someone to make me work and that someone was Bill!'

And work they certainly did. From February 1970, BBC Radio 2 broadcast thirteen *I'm Sorry I'll Read That Again* programmes, all scripted by Graeme

It's Whatever Turns You On.

and Bill. At the same time the team was hard at work on the second series of the Thames sitcom, *Doctor in the House*, writing all thirteen episodes that were to be screened from. By the time the series came to an end, on 3 July 1970, Graeme and Bill would be Goodies.

'It was only a reaction to *Monty Python* inasmuch as we had to admit that they had got the sketch show down to a fine art,' says Bill. '*The Goodies* was a reaction to them but not in the sense of a rival. Quite the opposite, actually. We were all great friends. And I was a fan of the show. We had seen *Python* do what we thought, and seemingly everybody in the world for the last thirty-odd years has thought, was the quintessential sketch show of all time. They had really done it absolutely spot-on and broken some conventions as well.'

Having been gently told by the Head of BBC Television Comedy, Michael Mills, that *Broaden Your Mind* had come to its natural end, Graeme, Bill and Tim put their heads together for a follow-up series. 'We were very much trying to continue what we had started in series two, but at the same time take it in a different direction,' recalls Tim. 'To that end we considered the title "Narrow Your Mind", simply to highlight that the two programmes were connected. It was the same people doing something slightly different.'

On 5 June 1970, Mills wrote a memo to Jack Beale in the BBC copyright department regarding 'Narrow Your Mind (Working Title)' and saying: 'I should be glad if you would negotiate a fee with Graeme Garden, Tim Brooke-Taylor and Bill Oddie as joint authors of a series of seven shows which (for want of a better title) we will call "Narrow Your Mind". They are to be recorded on 8 October and for six following weeks.' Indeed, BBC correspondence for the first series of *The Goodies* notes that the show was '(previously called "Narrow Your Mind")'.

An important meeting had been arranged for June 1970: 'Michael Mills was, unquestionably, one of the great patrons of *The Goodies*,' says Graeme. 'The three

Bill's historical concept sketch for what *The Goodies* should look like. Bill and Graeme are pretty much on the money.

of us went to him and said, "We want to do a show about an agency of three blokes who do anything, any time." It really was as simple as that. He said, "Well, I get that idea on my desk about twice a week!"'

'And,' notes Bill, 'before we had the chance to say "But…" and try and champion the idea, Mills himself said, "But I know and trust you three to come up with something different … so have a series!" Not have a pilot. Have a series! We were promised seven programmes and Mills really had no idea what we were going to deliver. We didn't have much of a clue ourselves!'

Graeme explains further: 'The basic idea was to incorporate the sort of comedy that we had all been using in sketches and sustain it for a half-hour programme. Bill and I had been working on the *Doctor in the House* shows and that was quite a traditional sitcom most of the time. We wanted to do a sitcom in the style of one of our sketches and present, what I think Bill called, "a concentrated half-hour of silliness"!'

'We had always worked in this two- or three-minute format,' agrees Bill. 'What I wanted to do was a half-hour story that used the sort of humour you would normally get in a sketch show. That's exactly what we did. In fact, to this day, it annoys me when someone comes up to me in the street and says, "I liked that sketch you did on *The Goodies*!" We never did sketches on *The Goodies*. The shows weren't sketches. They were a hybrid of the sketch and the sitcom, but undoubtedly half-hour shows that only worked as a whole.'

'We came up with "Super Chaps Three" as a title,' says Tim, 'and it was quite a good one because it was self-mocking and a nice Gerry Anderson takeoff.'

'But we quickly discarded it,' says Bill. 'I came up with "The Goodies" and it stuck. It sounded like a pop group, which was great for me, and it also had the ring of all those ITV crime-busting shows. You know, it was always *The Avengers* or *The Champions* or whatever.'

'I've always had reservations about "The Goodies",'

ASK ASPEL

Michael Aspel 'was a great champion of the show', according to Bill. 'He used to host this kid's request programme. They wrote in to him and asked to see their favourite television clips again. Our stuff was always on it.' Indeed, during November and December 1970 almost every edition of *Ask Aspel* featured *The Goodies* and the team were interviewed on the 18 December show. They were interviewed again on 7 September 1976 and answered children's questions.

'I'm sure the show helped heighten our profile,' reflects Bill. 'It probably made us appear to be even more like children's entertainers for some people at the BBC as well. So thanks, Michael!'

THE TRANDEM

The iconic mode of transport for the Goodies was in the series from the start, but 'it was something of an embarrassment for us', admits Tim. 'It was the first day of filming and we got on it to ride off but, of course, we couldn't. We couldn't ride it! So we rewrote the script to make it look like we were intending to fall off it!'

For Bill, 'That first bike was fine. I liked it because I didn't have to do anything. It was a normal tandem with an extra bit at the back where I sat, so there were no pedals on my bit. I just had to sit on it and laugh at the other two frantically pedalling! The second one was modified to have three sets of working pedals and you had to get your foot on at the right time or else you would ram the other two [pedals] into Tim and Graeme's shin. There was blood everywhere. I'm convinced that's why the thing is painted red – to conceal our blood!'

The team's unique mode of transport remains one of the show's most iconic images.

laments Tim. 'I just thought it sounded just too goody-goody really. We've had to live with it for over thirty years, but it worked and it still works, so I can't complain.'

'Bill and I wrote the scripts, but it was all three of us who were the Goodies,' says Graeme. 'It's just that Tim made less of a contribution to the script than us. Hence the "with…" writing credit.'

Tim explains that 'for that first series we certainly all sat down and created *The Goodies*. That notion wasn't even heard of in those days at the BBC, but I suppose if we had been in America we would have had a "series created by…" credit for all three of us. Graeme and Bill are incredibly good and incredibly fast writers. To be honest, I don't think I'm a good enough, quick enough writer.'

'We would take one week to write one episode,' confirms Graeme.

'I just couldn't keep up with their amazing output,' admits Tim. 'They also liked to go away and write the series on their own. They would divide the show up into two halves and each go away and write a half. That's why the "commercial break" was a handy device. It sort of meshed the two, sometimes very different, halves of the show together. My role, apart from offering odd lines and ideas, was to point out when one of their ideas didn't quite work. The three of us had to agree on everything and I was the deciding factor, I suppose!'

Fledgling Goodies: Tim the Toff…

And Bill the Bolshevik.

Open for Business. The Goodies set up shop in series 1, episode 1.

'It doesn't wrangle after all these years at all,' chuckles Bill. 'I don't mind Tim getting a writing credit for ten years and not doing a fucking thing to earn it! I certainly don't resent him for having about a third of the money for the writing either! That's fine!'

Amazingly, the team would sit in on planning and budget meetings at the BBC and be privy to the amount that each and every joke and pratfall was costing the corporation. 'That was a unique situation I would think!' claims Bill. 'And it wasn't as if we were demanding [to be at] these meetings, the BBC positively encouraged us. We were invited to all the planning discussions long before the filming began. I seem to remember planning meetings being postponed if one of the three of us couldn't make it!'

'It was also important to us that the show would have an underlying sense of seriousness,' remembers Graeme. 'We wanted very much to steer clear of preaching to an audience. We didn't want to force serious issues down people's throats, but we did want to tackle serious issues in a funny way. We would start a series with a long list of topics. Pollution. Sex equality. The cod wars. It looked like a wish list for *Panorama*. All we would do was take two elements and stick them together. Say, black-pudding-eating Northerners and the Martial Arts craze. Then you had a funny show!'

'It wasn't a comedy list at all,' confirms Bill. 'We used to have this way of coming up with these ideas. We would all meet at the beginning of the series and write down this whole list of topics, some of which were topical and some of which were areas we hadn't done before. It was a straight list. And, I hate to admit it, but Tim did come up with some of the suggestions! It would boil down to two lists. One was a cultural list – the fads and fashions of the time. The other was a list of subjects that interested us and that we hadn't done yet. It was just a case of putting contradictory ideas together. We did that time and time again.'

But perhaps the major breakthrough was to cast themselves as heightened versions of themselves. Tim was Tim. Graeme was Graeme. And Bill was Bill, who explains, 'I suppose that came from the Beatles films and the Monkees. They were playing themselves or, at the very least, characters that were being presented to the public as the "real" John Lennon and the like. If nothing else, *The Goodies* gave us a worldwide identity!'

'It isn't really like me at all,' insists Tim. 'Although I must admit I am a total coward. But that's the only trait I share with my character!'

'Tim is always moaning about the character we gave him,' chuckles Bill. 'Even to this day he says, "I never wear a suit!" and it's true, we never ever saw him in a suit and tie but, somehow, we always felt he *should* be wearing one. Anyway, look, he's the posh one with the silly double-barrelled name and the poncey blond hair. You're playing the right-wing, pro-royal wet, OK!'

'As for Graeme,' continues Bill, 'he's certainly cleverer than both Tim and myself. He's probably cleverer than Tim and myself combined! And he's always had that air of otherness about him, even at university. He's a qualified doctor, of course, and has that professorial thing going on. He knows what's what and what goes where!'

'I think my character could have saved the world!' claims Graeme.

'And as for me,' sighs Bill, 'I suppose, within the group, I'm the most reasonable one. I'm the righteous conservationist attacking the morals of the other two.'

For Tim, 'We all identified with Bill's character. He was very much the spokesman for what we all felt. In a way "Bill" is an accurate reflection of Bill himself and he certainly was the voice for how all the Goodies really felt about things.'

Pre-filming for the series began at the BBC Ealing Film Studios on 14 September 1970 and wrapped just under a month later. Three days earlier, the very first episode had gone in to studio to be recorded in front of a live audience. However, for the rest of the great British public and, indeed, the press, the whole series seemed to be under wraps.

Even the *Radio Times* seemed fairly vague as to what the programme was all about, describing Tim, Graeme and Bill as 'three of the Goodies . . . as opposed to the "baddies", they are a firm of three who lay themselves open to some very strange commissions'. Bill was giving little away when he revealed that: 'Tim is the respectable front man, Graeme plays the backroom boy who provides the clever stuff. And me, I'm the aggressive one.' But he was clear about one thing. 'We've made it very, very visual. There's lots of film and it's the sort of show – we hope – which couldn't possibly be done on radio.'

COMMERCIAL BREAKS

A popular element of the early *Goodies* shows, episode one features an effeminate Tim as the Fairy Puff Man failing to be waylaid by the 'grey, grey, grey' housewife (Maria O'Brien) as she strips away her dirty clothes for washing. Graeme promotes the Goodies Tea Set and insists, 'They were all rooted in reality to some extent.'

Indeed, on occasions, recalls Tim, 'We would have the same actor from the ad we were sending up. Milton Reid played my very butch bodyguard in a cigarette commercial in "Kitten Kong". He had been in the original advert.'

Both versions of 'Kitten Kong' featured Robinson's Heavy Duty Paper – so strong a car can't break through it. The original episode featured *Goodies* favourites Carol Roberts and Pat Gordeno as a couple of dolly birds in a Cathay Lather advert.

So forceful was the liquidated Golden Dairy margarine spurting from a refrigerator in 'Winter Olympics' that it drenched Tim's feminine alter ego and even knocked his wig off! He only had himself to blame, as director Jim Franklin recalls, 'I always thought they were Tim's ideas. In those days, I think we all knew, almost off by heart, all the classic commercials. So inspiration came from the originals.'

Nothing was as it seemed in a *Goodies* commercial. In 'The Stone Age', for example, Bristo Gravy gets rid of Graeme's Rolf Harris fast! But perhaps it was Tim's beans boy that made the biggest impact. Bill recalls, 'Those were based on the Heinz Baked Beans [adverts] and it was just an excuse to cover Tim in beans every other week!' The final comic commercial break came in 'The Race' at the end of series four, the event being marked with Tim's bean boy finally getting it right!

Series 1, Episode 1

THE TOWER OF LONDON

First broadcast: Sunday, 8 November 1970, 10 p.m.

Judging by the opening episode, it wasn't just the BBC, the media and the public who were uncertain what *The Goodies* was all about. The Goodies themselves seemed a little vague about it, too.

The script introduces the characters moving in to their new office thanks to a legacy from Tim's dearly departed auntie. Graeme has spent the money on a computer and impressive gadgetry, but it's Bill who pinpoints the fatal flaw. None of them knows what the Goodies do. Tim's rather sheepish suggestion that 'We do good to people!' is typically greeted with Bill's, 'How wet!', but soon a

message from the Black Rod (Gertan Klauber) provides them with their first assignment … from Buckingham Palace.

'Graeme and I wrote that as an introduction to the characters for the audience,' recalls Bill, 'but it was useful for us as well. It provided a reasonable opening to the business and set up this wonderfully vague notion of a new and challenging assignment each week. That was *The Goodies.* In the early days, at least.'

Because his men are wasting away for lack of beef, the Head Beefeater (George Baker) asks the team to protect the crown jewels. Looking back, Bill is amazed. 'We were called a kid's programme. In the first one we had drug references, tits and a royal scandal! If that's kid's television, it's pretty far-out kid's television!'

Torturous laughs as the Goodies face their first assignment.

'Are you alone?' 'No, there's three of us!'

'What?' 'Yes, we're alone. The three of us!'

Series 1, Episode 2

SNOOZE

First broadcast: Sunday, 15 November 1970, 10.30 p.m.

Assigned the task of promoting the latest sleeping powder, Graeme soon gets to work on a new, improved formula, "Snooze". Guinea pig Bill is launched on a hectic sleepwalking trip around town and soon the whole country is dropping off!

A timely comment on the all-powerful clout of advertising, this episode fully sets out Graeme's stall as the crazed scientist of the group. It's typified in his early morning wake-up call: a gentle tap from a mechanical hand, followed by a medicine ball hurtling towards his slumbering form. It continues with tea, breakfast, newspaper-reading and even dressing is made simple by what Graeme describes as 'the magic of science, dear boy!'

Playing hyper businessman Rupert Wincheater is Roddy Maude-Roxby who, in early 1969, had fronted the Terry Jones and Michael Palin comedy, *The Complete and Utter History of Britain*.

Tim remembered, 'When we first started filming *The Goodies*, it was two weeks before one of the crew – I think he was an electrician – laughed. That really depressed us at the time, but you get used to it. Of course, you're always laying yourself wide open and that's half the fun – though it still frightens me. We're always walking the knife-edge between being very funny and very silly, so when you do fall flat on your face, it is *awful*.'

Bill's hallucinogenic sherbet trips were a popular element of the early shows.

Series 1, Episode 3

GIVE POLICE A CHANCE

First broadcast: Sunday, 22 November 1970, 10.35 p.m.

Police Commissioner Butcher (Paul Whitsun-Jones) wants to improve his image, but Tim's cosy 1950s attitude towards the force is soon shattered by first-hand police brutality.

At a time when BBC television's presentation of the police was still typified by Jack Warner in *Dixon of Dock Green*, this was a hard-hitting, satirical dig. Particularly if you were young, hairy and short. As Tim reveals, 'This was more of Bill's mission. He didn't have good memories of the police.'

The show is deeply rooted in the late 1960s, with a Summer of Love-styled love-in, *Easy Rider* references and the Hell's Angels rejecting the idea of a free concert in Hyde Park. Even the courtroom resounds to the John Lennon inspired anthem, 'Give Police A Chance'.

Directing the series, Jim Franklin recalls his reaction to the first batch of scripts he was handed, 'The first word that springs to mind is "challenge". The Goodies had initially asked for my services to direct the film sequences in the first series. I had already worked with them before and they knew my reactions to their scripts would be largely in tune with their zany ideas. They knew I would not classify them as mad, because they already thought I was slightly mad myself.'

'You saw what they just did. They roughed us up.'

'Just force of habit or habit of the force.

Ha ha ha ... I wish I was dead!'

Series 1, Episode 4

CAUGHT IN THE ACT

First broadcast: Sunday, 29 November 1970, 10 p.m.

A post-Profumo scandal hits the British government when the Minister for Trade and Domestic Affairs (Mollie Sugden) is photographed at the Playgirl Club, an establishment that presents the male equivalent of the Bunny Girls – the Wolves!

Following on from the previous show, here we have a good copper, in the seductive shape of Liz Fraser as the undercover Playgirl Club manageress. In turn, Graeme infiltrates the club as a Wolf. 'I've got a vision – which isn't pleasing me one bit – of Graeme done up as a male bunny,' recalls Bill. 'He had this enormous lock over the serious parts down there with this big phallic key sticking out. The idea was that the woman could pay to unlock the secret. It doesn't bear thinking about really.'

Series 1, Episode 5

THE GREENIES

First broadcast: Sunday, 6 December 1970, 10.50 p.m.

Having checked the radioactive map of Britain, the Goodies head off on holiday to the Cornish village of Penrudden Cove. Reverend Rose (George Benson) is running the entire town and appeals for help to stop the military taking over.

The misguided threat in this episode are the jolly good chaps of the British army, headed by the Brigadier (Richard Caldicott: a regular figure of authority as Commander Povey on the long-running BBC radio comedy *The Navy Lark* since 1959) and his bemused second-in-command (Timothy Carlton). In a telling reflection on the tendency to put animals before people, the military reveal that the only complaint resulting from the destruction of the New Forest was the death of the ponies!

Naturally, it is Bill who is up in arms over the environmental situation, employing protest song and sex (a stripping Pauline Devaney) to bamboozle the enemy. But it's Graeme who succeeds in mixing up the plans for the proposed weapon depot with those for a children's playground.

'We heard strange rumblings and eerie voices up on Penrudden Hill. Poor old Jed Terdivick climbed up the hill to investigate. Gentlemen, he returned a raving, mindless idiot.' 'I remember old Jed Terdivick. He always was a raving, mindless idiot!'

Series 1, Episode 6

CECILY

First broadcast: Sunday, 13 December 1970, 10 p.m.

Desperate for work, the Goodies search the situations vacant, but Tim is too proud to tackle any home-help positions.

He then agrees to take the first job that is offered, and it turns out to be home help to a nervous and eccentric couple (Ann Way and Robert Bernal) who have left their home in the care of their young daughter, Cecily (Jill Riddick).

Tim remembers being 'in a dress having to do the job. Graeme dresses as a gardener and I dress as a nanny. It wasn't easy for the other two to play women of any sort with beards and muttonchops.'

Jim Franklin remembers, 'the script called for a large house to be blown up. Luckily an estate-agent friend of mine was about to demolish a large house to make way for a new development. If we timed it carefully, we would be able to pull the front of this house down, on cue, at the same time as a visual-effects explosion. As this was undoubtedly a "once only opportunity", I emphatically informed the cameraman that we would need two cameras for this shot. "Oh, alright," he said, testily. "But my Eclair camera never fails." On the day we ran an Eclair camera and an Arriflex side by side. The Eclair jammed! Just call me "Lucky Jim".'

'Tim was always the woman because Bill and I wrote it!' reveals Graeme. 'I sympathise with women', muses Tim. 'I would not like to wear their clothes every day.'

Series 1, Episode 7

RADIO GOODIES

First broadcast: Sunday, 20 December 1970, 9.45 p.m.

Dissatisfied with the General Post Office when they turn down the Goodies' application for a radio station, the Goodies decide to start their own pirate station, outside the five-mile limit, of course. Graeme goes berserk with power and introduces the Goodie-post, with disastrous results.

Not only that, but Graeme sets sail on the good ship *Saucy Gibbon* and starts broadcasting ... mainly German pianist Horst Jankowski's 1965 hit recording of 'A Walk in the Black Forest'!

Pirate radio stations had become illegal in August 1967 thanks to the Marine Offences Act. The Act prompted the most famous of them all, Radio Caroline, to broadcast from onboard ship and out of legal jurisdiction. Indeed, the draft script for this episode from August 1970 notes that the Americanised disc-jockey patter should be delivered 'à la Rosko', a reference to Emperor Rosko, one of Radio Caroline's broadcasters. The script also included a cut scene where Graeme explains that the wavelength 247 metres gives the best reception, before Bill knowingly points out that this is Radio 1's wavelength. Topically, Rosko had left Caroline and joined Radio 1 in September 1970, just three months before this episode was broadcast.

In terms of writing, this episode was the major group effort of the series. Bill largely wrote the first half centred on the postal service, Graeme wrote the end, and Tim made a major contribution: 'The best bits are mine!' he chuckles.

'It was the blueprint for what *The Goodies* would become,' believes Graeme. 'We all realised that we were becoming like *Batman*. The guest baddie would come in and we would just stand around feeding them lines.'

Bill explains that 'the idea was each week one of us would go bad and become the baddie. It was the obvious solution. One of us would provide the villainy and the other two would try and save the situation. It was great, because it allowed one of us to go totally over the top; usually me or Graeme. Tim seemed to retain his own type of sanity most of the time. His madness was to be even more normal or even more patriotic!'

Tim agrees: '"Radio Goodies" was the start of the classic *Goodies* format for want of a better word. Importantly, it helped us stamp out that notion of us being goody-goody all the time. We embraced this element of insanity within the group which the others had to try and contain!'

In this episode it is Graeme who takes on the mantle of mad genius. 'Of course,' reflects Graeme, 'we had to give my character's evil schemes a flaw so the others could defeat him. But I really knew how the plans could work!'

CRICKLEWOOD

The North London address of the Goodies was simply adopted because in 1970 both Tim and Graeme were living there. 'I was in the far posher Hampstead,' says Bill. Still, Bill immortalised the place in two songs, 'Cricklewood Shakedown' and the Beatlesque 'Cricklewood'. So powerful was the notion that the Goodies really did share a home there that the BBC would often be forwarded fan letters simply addressed to The Goodies, No Fixed Abode, Cricklewood

I'M SORRY I'LL READ THAT AGAIN

New Year Special

The seventh series of *I'm Sorry* ... had introduced Radio Prune, the central conceit allowing the team to indulge in half an hour of madness.

Produced by team member David Hatch, and Peter Titheradge, this special was recorded on 20 December 1970 at the Playhouse. It promised, according to a BBC memo, to include 'two new songs by Bill Oddie'.

The show presented the controversial concept of full-frontal radio in drag, the risqué Miss World contest, bawdy Christmas songs censored by the BBC, a comic review of the year and an epic retelling of *Dr Zhivago*. 'It really did attract a cult following,' recalls Tim, 'but we were all getting so tied up with other projects that the time had come to call it a day. Still, we all had a real loyalty to the show, even John.'

Cleese, who had always delighted in showing his contempt for the series, did indeed grit his teeth and rejoin the team for this special. 'John liked doing the show or else he wouldn't have done it!' confirms Bill. 'And he enjoyed the team. But he was doing *Python* on television and that's what he wanted to do. He got a bit tired of doing the silly puns Graeme and I were writing. We still loved writing it. I would have been happy writing it for years. It was just all those jokes that never failed to make us laugh. Still, there was something endearingly arrogant about John. By this stage, he had even had it written into his contract that he didn't have to come in to rehearse!'

with Tim Brooke-Taylor • John Cleese
Graeme Garden • David Hatch • Jo Kendall • Bill Oddie

Above: Material from the New Year Special was amongst that included in this 1985 publication.

Left: The series reached a new audience when the BBC Radio Collection began releasing cassette collections in 1990.

Right: The embryo of 'Lady Constance'. Tim in the Oscar Wilde sketch from Cambridge Circus as drawn by Humphrey Barclay.

A Circus or a Seaside Pier. A Sausage or a Can of Beer…

WILD THINGS

With *The Goodies* attracting almost two million loyal viewers on BBC2, producer John Howard Davies was in a congratulatory mood. On 23 November 1970, just four days after 'Radio Goodies' had been recorded, he wrote to Bill: 'Thank you so much for a lovely series. I enjoyed it thoroughly and, although we had our fair measure of problems, by and large I think we were successful. On reflection, it seems to me that the funnier shows did not really have a cause; Beefeaters, Snooze, Playgirl Club and the last one were funny because they were dotty and because, for once, they were entertaining for their own sake without the confusion of satire.' With tongue planted firmly in cheek, Davies happily anticipated a second series. 'I hope you will remember when you are writing it, that sex-starved producers as well as sex-starved actors, appreciate the occasional girls in the series.'

Fun For All the Family.

Davies wrote to Tim thanking him for his 'almost unfailing good humour and for helping me with the pronunciation of various Anglo-Saxon words and for being just as much a coward as I am. I look forward to next year with the usual mixture of hope, pessimism and plain old-fashioned fright.'

While Davies's letter to Graeme mentions the letter to Bill which 'no doubt he will show you', Davies continued: 'I must admit I enjoyed working with you immensely and am looking forward to putting up with your side whiskers for most of '71.'

Davies had already written to director Jim Franklin. 'Thank you so much Jim for all your work on *The Goodies*. It is doubtful whether anyone (except me!) could have done a better job than you did and, as you know, the boys consider the film as the star of the show. If I can ever afford you in the future, which I doubt, I hope we will work together again!'

Davies also sent notes to all his crew, notably editors Alan Lygo and Michael Rosenberg. 'I shall officially request both you gentlemen for the next series of *The Goodies* and can honestly say that you have made film editing, at least for me, a very different proposition to what it usually is. Now don't take that the wrong way, I mean it was actually pleasant and, I thought, splendidly done.'

Even more crucially, Robin Scott, the controller of BBC2, was equally impressed, in turn sending Davies a note reflecting that 'this is a delightful series. Sincere thanks and congratulations for the important part you have played in making it so.'

So it was hardly surprising when, with two episodes from the first series still awaiting transmission, a second series was commissioned in December 1970. By 25 February 1971, Roger Hancock was negotiating the writing credits: 'Naturally, the manner in which this is presented on the screen will depend on what form the credits take, but as long as Messrs. Garden and Oddie receive the principal credit and Mr. Brooke-Taylor a subsidiary one, they will all be satisfied.' The alphabetical order for performance was presumed from the previous series. Internally referred to as 'The Goodies II', a further thirteen episodes were requested, with filming to be split into two recording blocks. Location work on the first block started at the end of May and continued unabated until August, by which time BBC1 had run a complete repeat season of the first seven episodes. Even more successful than on their first screening, the viewing figures peaked at over four million.

Bill's sherbet trips were dropped after series one although he has a crafty suck in 'The Movies'.

Still, the Goodies weren't having everything their own way. It had been requested that Bill's drug-like sherbet trips be dropped from the show. 'I wouldn't say I was angry exactly, but I was disappointed!' remembers Bill. 'I just quite liked the sherbet visions actually! I'm certain that if we had been an American series that element would have been kept in. Kept in without question as a continuing factor that audiences could expect to see. Every week you would have had me enjoying the sherbet trip whatever the plot. But maybe it was for the best. We always liked the challenge of thinking up new ideas. We never tried to rely on a gimmick for the laughs. We liked to try different things as much as possible, so I suppose the BBC forced Graeme and I to think up something new!'

'We had also earned a bit of team spirit,' continues Bill, 'insomuch as we began to build up our own repertory company of extras. They can seriously bugger things up. A lot of extras are absolutely dreadful. All they seemed to care about was getting more money. More money than the star of the show in some cases. And food. They were always the first people at the tuck wagon when a break was called and we were left standing at the back of the queue waiting for the leftovers! All the extras do is stand around gawping at what's going on and they can seriously wreck the atmosphere of a shoot. But anyway, we had a very good team of people and the *Goodies* nerd can spend many happy hours watching the programmes and trying to spot the same faces time after time. They were very important to the show.' Bill admits that, 'Looking back on our early days, I can't believe we did some of those things. I look at some of the old episodes and wonder what the hell we were doing.'

But, as Graeme says, 'Back in the old days the BBC was very supportive of new TV shows. If your first series wasn't that great, they would trust you enough to grow and develop into the second one. It wouldn't have happened with the commercial companies, because if you didn't get the ratings straightaway, you were out.'

JOHN HOWARD DAVIES

(1939–)

As a child actor he starred as Oliver Twist in David Lean's definitive version and, in 1951, played the eponymous hero of *Tom Brown's Schooldays*. From the mid-1960s, he entered television as the producer of such comedy favourites as *All Gas and Gaiters*, *The World of Beachcomber* and the first four episodes of *Monty Python's Flying Circus*. He produced the first two series of *The Goodies* and handled studio direction. Later, he produced the 1972 series of *Steptoe and Son*, the first series of *Fawlty Towers* and all of *The Good Life*. In the late 1980s, he worked as an executive producer at Thames Television and oversaw the death of *The Benny Hill Show* and the birth of *Mr Bean*.

Series 2, Episode 1

SCOTLAND

First broadcast: Friday, 1 October 1971, 9.20 p.m.

The Goodies save a suicidal zookeeper and meet a canny Scot.

A high calibre of guest actors was retained and, for Tim, 'It was a real thrill to be working with people we had admired for years. Stanley Baxter was a particular favourite.' Baxter, whose last series of *The Stanley Baxter Show* had finished the previous February, was dubious of the script's depiction of the Scots. He finally accepted it as a playful viewpoint of the typical Englishman and gamely went over the top with a performance based on the manic arched eyebrows of *Dad's Army* regular John Laurie. With a ramshackle Loch Ness Monster and a giant bagpipe spider, Baxter's ebullient performance is almost subtle in comparison.

'We found out that no one was actually asking the performers we wanted because they thought they would be too expensive,' says Tim, 'so we went straight to the artistes' agents and put it to them. Most of the people did the programme simply because they wanted to be in *The Goodies*.' The zookeeper desperate to find a monster to fill his monster enclosure proved tempting enough for

Bernard Bresslaw to accept. Fresh from filming *Carry On At Your Convenience*, Bresslaw's most recent television credits had ranged from the lead monster in *Doctor Who* ('The Ice Warriors') to a playful Frankenstein's monster in *Carry On Christmas*.

In 'Scotland', it is Baxter who is the mysterious monster, emerging from the Nessie skin after giving Graeme the willies on the loch!

The second series attracted more of the best actors on British television with both Bernard Bresslaw and Stanley Baxter enlivening the series opener.

Series 2, Episode 2

COMMONWEALTH GAMES

First broadcast: Friday, 8 October 1971, 9.20 p.m.

Nobody in their right mind would consider the Goodies as sportsmen, but when their country needs them to save the Commonwealth, they rally round the flag.

A knowing satire on the failure of British sportsmen upon the world stage, Tim lets rip with a patriotically charged speech about cricket and beating 'Johnnie Foreigner'. The Minister of Sports (Reginald Marsh) is a typical depiction of gruff British authority, pitting the trio against the August Bank Holiday Islands.

With the prize being the entire Commonwealth, it is first suggested that important aged Members of Parliament should take on the task, but they fail the sex test ... a test the Goodies easily pass with the help of the shapely secretary Miss Foster (Valerie Stanton). 'And that was the least energetic part of the filming,' says Bill.

Indeed, to the refrains of Bill's 'Superman' song, the trio were put through their paces during a comic physical work-out. 'We loved the fact the show was being compared to classic cartoons,' continues Bill. 'But in a way we regretted it because we began to think of ourselves as cartoon characters and it set ourselves up to be treated as human props. More to the point, it set us up in the eyes of the public as something not quite real. We were treated like some sort of animated character and that could get quite disconcerting. No one seemed to treat us like real actors ... perhaps we weren't!'

'Most definitely, most of the Goodies visual trickeries on film were based directly on the works of Keaton, Lloyd and indeed Chaplin,' says Jim Franklin. 'The Goodies used every silent film trick ever invented. Sometimes the action was even shot in reverse to achieve the desired effect.'

Series 2, Episode 3

POLLUTION

First broadcast: Friday, 15 October 1971, 10.10 p.m.

The Goodies take on the environment and clean up Britain.

Graeme's computer predicts that the world will end on Monday thanks to pollution, with another efficient figure of British politics emerging in the shape of Mr Eastbourne, the Minister of Pollution (Ronnie Stevens). The ultimate authority figure is revealed as David Frost.

Director Jim Franklin had honed his Midas touch by debunking authority figures although he modestly explains that: 'I think "Midas" touch would be to overstate my abilities somewhat. However, Tim and Graeme knew that I was originally a film editor who had a leaning towards comedy and "quirky" films. Initially I had worked for Robert Robinson on *Points of View* in the 1960s. I had been responsible for making Sir Malcolm Sergeant appear to be conducting The Beatles in concert singing 'She Loves You'. I had been doing a form of film editor's "cartooning" in response to viewers' letters. One viewer asked how it was that all dignitaries seemed to be so loquacious. I responded with a viciously edited sequence where many famous dignitaries, politicians, Church leaders and military men could only stutter and say "um and "er" for about thirty seconds, one after the other.'

The scene as the Goodies ride through a field while being pelted by dead birds falling from the sky is a chilling image indeed. There is no dialogue and certainly no laughs in this moment as the trandem trio realise they are well and truly needed.

'Anything *is* possible! You can achieve anything on television if you're prepared to pay for it.' Graeme.

Series 2, Episode 4

THE LOST TRIBE

First broadcast: Friday, 22 October 1971, 10.10 p.m.

When a lady in distress (Bridget Armstrong as Hazel Knutt) appeals to the Goodies to help rescue her father (Roy Kinnear's 'Professor' Knutt), she leads them into danger in the Amazon jungle, among the Bu-Boom people of the Orinoco.

Structured like an Arthur Conan Doyle adventure yarn on a budget, the travel-diary entries are narrated by Graeme, who winces when the episode is mentioned. 'It was all about a missing professor who discovers a lost tribe who shout "bu-boom" after every corny old joke!'

'It certainly didn't get much of a reaction from the studio audience,' recalls Tim, 'and Roy Kinnear, bless him, would try every trick he could to get a reaction.'

Roy Kinnear rocketed to stardom as part of David Frost's team in *That Was The Week That Was* in 1963. It made him a star of satire although he was all ready well known in the business thanks to his association with Joan Littlewood's Theatre Workshop. In 1962 he had appeared in Littlewood's film, *Sparrows Can't Sing*, and director Richard Lester cast him in a handful of sixties classics, including the Beatles romp *Help!*. By the time of his Goodies debut he had appeared in the Hammer horror, *Taste the Blood of Dracula* and *Willy Wonka and the Chocolate Factory*, in a cast including Tim. Ever energetic, Roy Kinnear gives his all for this episode, also known as 'The Lost Tribe of the Orinoco'.

And Graeme, ever the skilful impersonator, dishes up a *soupçon* of television's Galloping Gourmet, Graeme Kerr.

'The *Sun* did a whole item on my hair. They said "the minute you change your hair Fleet Street jumps!"'. Tim.

Series 2, Episode 5

THE MUSIC LOVERS

First broadcast: Friday, 29 October 1971, 10.10 p.m.

When every musician in the country is stolen by The Maestro (Henry McGee), the Goodies work in harmony to put matters right.

Gangster tactics are combined with musical inspiration as the team throw brickbats at a glut of vinyl stars, whether it's *The Best of Rolf Harris* being a blank disc, or Cilla Black – who provides her own voice – setting Bill's teeth on edge. Even the recently disbanded Beatles get a mention as a studio door opens to the sound of an argument and a tossed-out guitar!

Although this was an episode close to Bill's heart, it was written just like any other *Goodies* show, as he explains: 'Graeme would write half and I would write half. Sometimes one of us would write all the visuals and the other would write all the dialogue bits, but it worked out to be roughly half and half. I was always very intimidated by Graeme's stuff. His would be beautifully typewritten and mine was scribbled down by hand. I could never really bring myself to criticise any of his stuff or change it, because I didn't want to spoil this immaculately presented piece of work!'

And director Jim Franklin was suitably in tune with what made the programme run smoothly. 'To understand a Goodies script is to know you will be making a programme that will embrace most of the elements of a *Tom and Jerry* cartoon, coupled with almost all the tricks used in silent movies *à la* Buster Keaton, Harold Lloyd and Charlie Chaplin' he explains.

'I've always maintained that our programmes may or may not be funny, but they're always interesting.' Bill.

Series 2, Episode 6

CULTURE FOR THE MASSES

First broadcast: Friday, 5 November 1971, 10.10 p.m.

The Goodies try to stop the mass export of Britain's antiques, hindered by the Minister of Culture (Julian Orchard), an auctioneer (Tommy Godfrey) and a millionaire Texan (Ray Marlowe).

With Sotheby's turned into a Cockney marketplace, Tim gets typically hot under the collar about the buyers: 'But they're not art lovers, they're Americans!' A satirical edge is made even sharper thanks to Bill's song, 'Philistine'.

Their assignment is to make art 'fun' and reverse the shameful situation of art galleries with no visitors but, by the end of the show, Graeme is happily selling a never-ending supply of *Monarch of the Glen*!

Tim displays his enigmatic smile!

KITTEN KONG

First broadcast: Friday, 12 November 1971, 10.10 p.m.

When the Goodies turn to matters veterinary, Graeme invents a new super pet food. 'Promotes rapid growth,' he claims … right up to the ceiling?

Arguably the most fondly remembered episode, Graeme laments, 'I can't stand watching "Kitten Kong" because that's the one everyone keeps banging on about. I don't say it doesn't make me chuckle, though!'

Often delighting in abusing animals, this tribute to our furry friends actually begins with Bill lovingly dishing up a slap-up meal for a stressed-out guinea pig. 'We soon get back to mistreating animals, though,' says Bill. 'I have distinct memories of trying to squash that bloody huge dog in the basket.'

But it was the kitten, provided by Graham Worswick, that won the hearts of the nation. Indeed, a memo from Jim Franklin's assistant, Carol Bunyan, reveals that, along with the Goodies themselves, 'Worswick (and cat)' had a dressing room in which to relax before the show. Moreover, Worswick received six tickets to the recording, with Bunyan signing off: 'My love to "Kong" – and I hope you enjoy the show.'

The cat was at its funniest in the 'Dumb Animals Exercise' sequence filmed behind Ealing Studios in Ealing Park, when he was 'basically a bit of fluff on a stick!' Bill explains, 'I'm happy to say that Ronnie Barker turned down the piece of material where Tim takes the kitten for a walk. The original idea was just that it was a very strong kitten that was to lead the walker a

Sketches for the Kong blue screen action and a Goodies mouse suit.

merry dance round a park. I wrote the bulk of that as a three-minute bit for Ronnie several years before and he dismissed it completely. To be fair to Ronnie, I always tended to do visual pieces for him and, bless him, he actually came up to me and said, "Look, it's very funny, but I just can't do this! I'm simply not fit enough!" There was obviously far too much running around for his liking! If he hadn't said that, Graeme and I might not have followed through with the idea and come up with the giant kitten. Who can tell! But I thought at the time, "OK, Ronnie, fair enough. I'll file that away and use it later!" Sure enough, I put it into "Kitten Kong" and it worked great. Nothing was wasted!'

Unfortunately for Tim, it provided one of his most uncomfortable moments on the show: 'Everything was filmed in stop-motion so I would be on the floor hanging on to the kitten, they would film that and I would then move a little bit, they would film that, and so on. Of course, you had to keep in the same place or else it wouldn't look right when it was cut together. In between filming a sequence of the kitten dragging me around the park, a dog came along and did its business right in front of me. I had no choice but to lie there and gradually move myself over it!'

Graeme remembers a 'particularly good audience' for the show and one that laughed in the right places, regardless of how many times the scene demanded retakes. 'Sometimes they laughed in the wrong places! The scene where I put the "special" suit on took three takes and that's why we

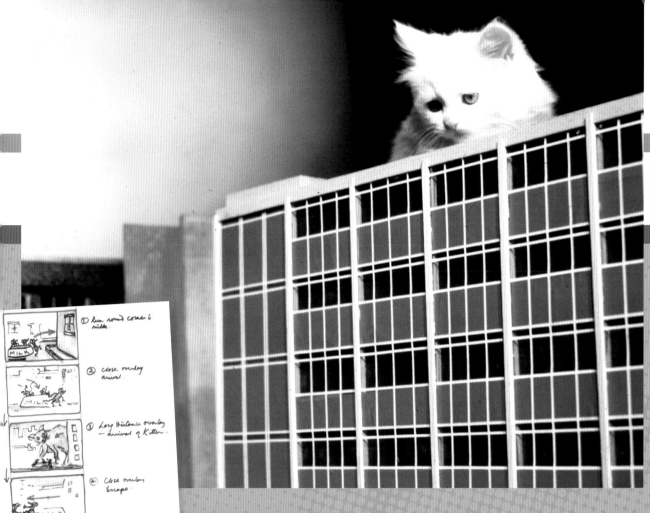

Jim Franklin's storyboard illustrates how painstakingly planned Twinkle's rampage was.

get a huge audience reaction when I finally manage it.' And all the studio tricks gelled perfectly, notably when 'Graeme' enters the quick-change cabinet and emerges immediately clad in his mouse suit. 'It wasn't me who went in you see,' reveals Graeme, 'it was a lookalike, and I was in the cabinet, in my mouse suit, waiting to take the huge needle off of my stand-in. Hence the seamless crossover.'

It achieves what the team wanted: a human cartoon. And the reference to that legacy is lovingly suggested. 'We recreated that classic moment of the Negro cook or nursemaid or whatever she is, standing on a chair, screaming at the mouse. That was pure Tom and Jerry.'

And, as Bill continues, 'We always tried to incorporate what I call "cartoon logic". You know, when there's a chase in a cartoon, whether it's a Tom and Jerry or a Roadrunner, the character is always going to run over the edge of a tall building or the edge of a mountain or something. The character keeps on running and they get to about seven or eight foot out. It's "cartoon logic" that you don't fall until you realise that there's nothing underneath you. It's the whole thing of looking down, looking into camera and the realisation – "Uh oh" – and then they fall down. We were trying to do that dressed up as mice for "Kitten Kong". We were working out what sort of wires we would need to lower us down against a blue screen and, after a while, everybody was getting really cheesed off – pun intended! This was when the other two finally realised my sense of reality had departed. I said, "Wait a minute, look it's not really on top of a big building is it?" They said, "No, it's a mock-up. It's only about four or five or six foot off the ground. No more than that!" I said, "Well, if it's only six foot off the ground that's fine. We won't need wires. We won't hurt ourselves. We can just do it ourselves!" I had finally lost it! But, the weird thing is … we did!'

Series 2, Episode 8

COME DANCING

First broadcast: Friday, 19 November 1971, 10.10 p.m.

Our heroes find treachery in the tango and villainy at the *valse* when they enter the bitter cut, thrust and natty reverse of a formation dance championship.

With a renewed craze for ballroom dancing and the celebrity-fodder media junket of *Strictly Come Dancing*, this is as topical as ever it was. *Goodies* regular Roland MacLeod plays Peter Vest, an unsubtle parody of *Come Dancing* host Peter West, who had presented the show since 1957 and who would bow out in 1972, less than a year after this programme's transmission. Television was clearly the major original target for the show, with the draft script containing an unused scene where Graeme

The Goodies relax on location, while the first ladies of British comedy, June Whitfield and Joan Sims, go head to head.

'Ballroom dancing is an oasis of dignity in the sterile waste of popular culture...'

'What a load of old rubbish.'

FARM FRESH FOOD

First broadcast: Friday, 10 December 1971, 10.10 p.m.

With its investigation into the notion of artificially altered food, this picked up on similar themes from 'Kitten Kong' and seems way ahead of its time today, where kitchens are run by chemists rather than chefs and everything comes out of a tin or a packet.

Bill mourns the demise of real food, while the supercilious waiter (Frank Thornton) of Ye Olde Shepherd's Cottage Restaurant, frowns upon fresh food and promotes the 'tasty' alternative.

John Le Mesurier as Tim's Uncle Tom is at the heart of the demoralising situation, but his performance is so vague and unassuming that his final redemption is all the more pleasing. And Jim Franklin – 'brilliant as always' according to Tim – displays his editing prowess with a hilarious sequence featuring dancing chickens!

This had stemmed from when, as Jim explains, he had been, 'working in Light Entertainment as a Film Associate. I created a mad film sequence that caused Harold Wilson, George Brown and Edward Heath to appear to be dancing the "Hokey Pokey" together. This was done by "reanimating" suitable newsreel footage to fit the music. Subsequently making live action dogs sing a duet in *Broaden Your Mind* had perhaps concluded my apprenticeship for working with the Goodies.'

'I found it very challenging, very exciting. Right from the word go, we were experimenting and we were enthusiasts.' Jim Franklin

criticises Tim's ballroom viewing habit and suggests a small-screen alternative. Something more cultural, like 'The Six Wives of Queen Victoria' or 'So You Think You Know All About the Elements of Formal Logic'. The BBC had screened *The Six Wives of Henry VIII* in 1970, while Raymond Baxter (a *Goodies* guest in 'It Might As Well Be String') had presented an ongoing *So You Think …* series of programmes since 1965. Bill, moreover, was to have been watching an *Avengers* rip-off, 'The Mutilators', where 'Emma gets torn slowly into little pieces, and Steed gets a harpoon in the lower abdomen'.

Still, as it turned out, there was more than enough violence on the dance floor, with rivals Penelope Fey (June Whitfield) and cigar-chewing Delia Capone (Joan Sims) battling for supremacy. Future Benny Hill and Russ Abbot stooge, Bella Emberg, can be spotted as part of Capone's mob.

Sometimes simply referred to as 'Dancing' in the BBC files, this episode has also been called 'Wicked Waltzing'.

Series 2, Episode 10

WOMENS LIB

First broadcast: Friday, 17 December 1971, 10.10 p.m.

A positive look at the feminist movement;
Gaye Brown as the Women's Libber is clearly
representing Germaine Greer.

'That was something I felt very strongly about,' says Bill.
'Women were still perceived as almost second-class
citizens in the show-business circles we were moving in.
Even the Pythons and Spike Milligan didn't know what
to do with them except use them as sex objects. It was a
sort of throwback to Cambridge, really. People like Miriam
Margolyes and Eleanor Bron had been in the Footlight
shows, but they weren't allowed into the Footlights Club! It
was like some appalling male preserve. It really annoyed me.
We used to have "ladies night" and that sort of thing. It was
like the Masons! Some people – yes, Tim, I'm talking about
you – actually voted against having women in the club!'

Tim tries to defend himself: 'It wasn't a sexist thing at all.
It was actually actresses at Cambridge who were involved
in the Amateur Dramatic Society and who were trying to
make the Footlights Club an extension of that. That's what
I didn't like. And, more importantly, I think we felt a bit
embarrassed. We were all young men and everybody got very
self-conscious where women were concerned. Our job was to
be very silly people. Women were less willing to make fools
of themselves and when they were around it made it hard for
the men as well … if you follow me!'

Still, Tim was made to pay for his earlier thoughts
as the script cast him as the maid Timbellina. Slapped
about and treated like a love slave by Allan Cuthbertson,
who actually believes Tim to be a woman, the shy young
thing – a sort of youthful Lady Constance – is reduced to
calling him 'master'. A love-crazed Graeme, meanwhile,
happily prances through the woods with his beloved
computer, having just been delivered in a Southern
Electronics Transport Company van!

Series 2, Episode 11

GENDER EDUCATION

First broadcast: Friday, 31 December 1971, 9.35 p.m.

'We had received a telegraph from Mary Whitehouse [Honorary General Secretary of the National
Viewers' and Listeners' Association] thanking us
for the very nice show we were doing,' remembers
Tim.

'We were appalled,' says Bill, 'so we decided
to make a show that she would absolutely
hate.' To that end, they created the whiter-
than-white Desiree Carthorse (Beryl Reid), who
commissions the Goodies to make a sex-education film
from her own script, 'How to Make Babies By Doing
Dirty Things'. Tim, Graeme and Bill give a memorable
three-way performance as 'dial-a-moaning backbench
Member of Parliament' Sir Reginald Wheelbarrow.
Character star Richard Wattis, set to return to TV as
Eric Sykes's neighbour Mr Brown in *Sykes*, was cast as
the interviewer.

In essence, the episode is a mixture of what *The
Goodies* was and what *The Goodies* would become,
inasmuch as a guest star with an assignment was
involved *and* one of the Goodies – this time Bill
– goes mad with power and takes over the 'baddie'
mantle from the guest. His sex- and violence-crazed

'I don't find you reading dirty books, looking at filthy
television programmes and playing around with girls. You
are obviously…' 'Unlucky!'

MRS DESIREE CARTHORSE.

Remnants from the BBC written archive illustrate the grue-some themes of Sinderella and the 'look' of the misguided client.

director puts together a production of 'Sinderella' with a suitably dominatrix performance from Valerie Stanton.

The 'Sets for Destruction' scene was aided by extensive notes and diagrams from Graeme. When the team were 'behind the three cottages', there would be steps up to a catwalk, 'so we can appear at the windows. If possible, when the set falls forward – remove steps and catwalk so that the only thing left standing is the pole, with Bill clinging to the top...'

The whole feel should be 'all very pantomimey and "flat"'.

The finale saw Bill blow up the BBC TV Centre in Wood Lane. 'Everyone who's worked there has felt like blowing the place up at some point or another,' he says. 'We did! That clip was screened at some BBC evening and got the biggest cheer of the night!'

'But we still didn't get a complaint from Mary Whitehouse,' moans Tim.

Series 2, Episode 12

CHARITY BOUNCE

First broadcast: Friday, 7 January 1972, 10.10 p.m.

'This was the episode that finally saw me really lose it!' reveals Bill.

'The show was becoming the guest villain with the three of us just standing in a row and almost becoming one voice of purity! Me, pure? I was very fed up about that! And in terms of us as a team, it drastically cut down the chance for interplay between us, which I've always thought was our greatest strength. To be honest it started to get to me a bit. I got very cross about it. We always seemed to end up in this situation where the character that came in to give the Goodies the assignment became the enemy of the Goodies and, from a purely practical point as writers, we gave them all the best lines. The baddie always gets the best lines, be it Walt Disney films, Charles Dickens novels or *The Goodies*!'

The guest star here, Freddie Jones, had recently distinguished himself as the creature in Hammer Films' *Frankenstein Must Be Destroyed* and as the nautical officer in *Doctor in Trouble*. 'He was very good in the show,' recalls Bill, 'it's just that we had absolutely no idea what he was going to do next. I remember that in rehearsal he didn't seem to remember two consecutive words for the whole of the session. We didn't have the faintest idea what he was doing. On the programme it sort of made sense with edits and our reactions and the like, but I suppose that's what made me finally snap about having guests in. We really didn't know what he was talking about most of the time! He couldn't remember the lines and he covered it up with this wide-eyed bluster. He covered it up rather brilliantly, it has to be said, but it was almost impossible to perform because of it.'

As the corrupt chairman of the Sparkipegs toothpaste factory – complete with a teeth-inspired desk designed by David Jones – Freddie asks the Goodies to take part in a promotional sponsored walk between London and Brighton. With Arthur Minion (Jonathan Cecil) and Miss Simpkins (Gilly McIvor) aiding and abetting, the wheeze is eventually changed to a sponsored charity bounce around the world – with the Goodies encased in giant toothpaste tubes.

'That really is us in those toothpaste tubes,' promises Bill. 'It may seem that anybody can dress up as a toothpaste tube and bounce on a spacehopper, but they can't! There are special skills that are required and you have to do it in a funny way! Talk about reflecting the seventies. Everyone seemed to have a spacehopper at the time and I wrote a song especially for the show called 'Spacehopper', as a matter of fact. They were usually orange with these great big phallic ears that you had to hang on to. They certainly weren't designed for Cambridge graduates in their thirties, but we did our best!'

With the bounce a success, it is revealed that the chosen charity, the Grieving Grannies Fund, is a tax dodge. Aggrieved, the Goodies – still in their toothpaste tubes – jump out of the window and bounce off. 'It was probably the most uncomfortable, physically, of all the shows,' says Bill. 'To keep those bloody tubes upright you had to have a harness over your shoulders and a metal plate was placed on top of your head. If you got out of sync during the bounce, it would hurt like hell. This thing would crash down giving you an instant lobotomy. Thank God it was filmed like a silent movie, because the noise of the three of us bouncing along was a constant stream of "Oh, Christ! … Oh, shit! … Oh, bugger!"'

Series 2, Episode 13

THE BADDIES

First broadcast: Friday, 14 January 1972, 10.15 p.m.

As if to send up their image once and for all, the Goodies put themselves down as favourites in the running for The Nicest Person in the World competition.

Although the police (represented by John Junkin) are on the case, the devious Dr Wolfgang Aldophous Rat-Phink Von Petal (Patrick Troughton) creates evil android Goodies to scupper the team's chances.

Having relinquished the lead role in *Doctor Who* in 1969 and returned to the fold of Hammer Films to play Christopher Lee's whipping boy in *Scars of Dracula*, Troughton was back as a much-in-demand jobbing actor and clearly relished the opportunity to give a lip-smacking performance. 'He just knew how to do it,' recalls Bill. 'Some of the straight actors that came in would say, "Oh, this is comedy is it, darling!" and do it all with big gestures and overacting. We would have to say, "Calm down a bit. Just play it for real."'

This episode is also referred to as 'Double Trouble'.

'Why doesn't anybody like us?' 'Fishface!'

'Well they ought to like us because we're

very nice to people.' 'Squirt!'

'We've never done anything wrong in all our lives.'

'Pansy!'

GOODY LOCATIONS

While filming in Maidenhead, Tim sustained a deep cut to his right knee when, as the medical report detailed, 'as part of the action the artist was required to fall over trandem'. The wound was washed, a plaster was applied and Tim was taken to hospital for an anti-tetanus injection. 'Kitten Kong' was largely filmed on location in the streets of Ealing in June and July of 1971. Number 13 Kerrison Place was used during the Loony Animal sequence with the real owner, Mrs R. Hopper, being advised that 'our effort on this occasion will consist of a lady [Anne Lee] coming out of the front door with a domestic pet (a stuffed snake in fact) and handing it over at the gate to an actor [Bill Oddie] dressed as an RSPCA Inspector.' The fishmongers, H.W. Critchett, at 132 South Ealing Road, was, as production assistant Donald Clive explained, required for 'a short sequence outside your shop. The shop is supposed to be empty, a giant cat having consumed all the fish. We would want to place one of our own artistes, dressed as a fishmonger [Freddie Payne], beside the slab, on which would be displayed a large fish skeleton.' Other locations used during Kitten Kong's rampage included the Ealing Technical College and The Borderers Rugby Football Club in Harefield.

ENGELBERT WITH THE YOUNG GENERATION

… and the Goodies who, with the second series pretty much in the can, accepted a recurring guest appearance on this BBC1 variety show hosted by the smooth singer Engelbert Humperdinck and co-produced by the German station, ZDF. The first of the Goodies inserts was recorded in the BBC studio TC8 on 10 December 1971, just before studio recording for 'Charity Bounce'. Broadcast on Sunday, 9 January, just two days after that episode, the programme had the star of the show assigning the Goodies to various tasks. The first, 'Pets', sees the singer hire the trio for walkies and link in to the Dumb Animals romp from 'Kitten Kong'. The majority of the subsequent appearances would follow suit, with programme two seeing his desire for an open-air concert sated by a clip from 'The Music Lovers'. Programme three has the Goodies keeping fit on his behalf thanks to the Superman section from 'Commonwealth Games'. Programme four features Humperdinck going to the Goodies for help with posting letters. En route he greets an aged postman (Albert Ward) delivering his original letter asking for their help two years previously! This link leads into the Pirate Postal Service sequence from 'Radio Goodies'.

The fifth show has Graeme curing Humperdinck's insomnia by playing his own hit recording of 'The Last Waltz'. It only succeeds in sending Bill on the sleepwalking escapade from 'Snooze'. And the sixth show reveals that he's busy for the next thirty-seven years and so has to hire the Goodies to look after his 'Farm Fresh Food'. All five of the linking sections were recorded during the same studio session assigned for 'The Baddies'.

The other programmes included *The Goodies* in specially filmed inserts. These were all linked by Humperdinck in the guise of an agony uncle answering viewers' questions and were recorded at the BBC television theatre on 20 February 1972. Programme seven attracts the question, 'Why are the Goodies called the Goodies?' leading into Good Deed Day – Babies. Programme eight revealed that: 'A lot of people have written to ask, "How do the Goodies move so fast?" Well, they have a very

unusual contract with the BBC. They get paid by the mile. So they really have to put in a lot of hard training.' This introduces the Gymnasium sequence. The thirteenth programme, closing the series on 2 April 1972, had Humperdinck reading a letter from the mothers of the Goodies requesting something for the older generation. He obliges with Pan's Grannies.

Although the programme was produced by Stewart Morris,

these specially filmed *Goodies* inserts were produced and directed by their regular collaborator Jim Franklin. They were subsequently resurrected as a compilation programme, 'A Collection of Goodies', in September 1972, although two sketches were not included. Programme nine showcases the government education film 'The Country Code' and programme twelve sees the team as bodyguards, using Humperdinck's picture as a dartboard and spending more time protecting his own cardboard cut-out!

'It wasn't far off how we felt about Engelbert,' remembers Bill. 'We were always having a go at him somehow or other. Tim and I do a drunken version of "Please Release Me" in "The End" and our first record suggests he needs to be looked at by a tree surgeon!'

The Goodies demonstrate exactly what they think of Engelbert's vocal prowess!

KITTEN KONG Montreux 1972 Edition

First broadcast: Sunday, 9 April 1972, 10.05 p.m.

Exactly a week after the last *Engelbert and the Young Generation* had aired, the Goodies were back in a newly polished presentation of the series two classic. David Gower, of the BBC copyright department, wrote to agent Roger Hancock explaining that:

John Howard Davies has informed me that the BBC is entering an episode of The Goodies *in the 1972 Montreux Festival. This programme is to be a virtual re-make of Programme 7 in the series, which was originally transmitted on the 12 November, 1971. For this festival version we should like to commission Graeme Garden, Bill Oddie and Tim Brooke-Taylor to re-write one-third of the dialogue and action, although the basic plot of the episode will remain the same. For this material I suggest a joint fee of £260.00, giving the BBC the right to use it for the first domestic transmission...*

The Goodies were interviewed about their chances at Montreux on *Nationwide* on 25 February 1972 and, just three days later, John Howard Davies accepted their revised script.

The re-filming was completed over a four-day schedule from 26 February 1972 and, according to Tim, added 'fifty per cent more Twinkle footage!' It also added Michael Aspel, who had been referred to as Michael Aspirin in 'The Baddies'.

'He was up for it on "Kitten Kong",' says Bill. 'That giant kitten's paw crushing him is a great moment. It took him thirty years to get his own back on me on *This Is Your Life*!'

'We just added a few new things to the old show,' continues Bill. 'Things that we thought would impress the judges. The end is more visual. And I'm pretty certain we added Jim Franklin's singing dogs as well.'

Tim remembers: 'Jim's "singing dogs" first appeared on *Broaden Your Mind* and was resuscitated for the Montreux entry of "Kitten Kong". The "singing dogs" were shot in Jim's back garden and the secret of making them look as if they were mouthing the words was, as Jim put it, to feed them lots of toffees. No animals were

With the 'star' of the show and model Rosemarie Chalmers.

'We've got to find him and catch him before he eats someone he shouldn't.'

'Ah, you mean something he shouldn't.'

'I know what I mean.'

hurt in the filming.'

But Michael Mills wasn't amused. He was determined that *The Goodies* shouldn't lose sight of its family appeal and, in a letter sent to John Howard Davies, he said:

> *I saw* The Goodies *the other day, the one about Kitten Kong. It is very funny and very well produced, but... There is one 'bleeding', one 'bloody' and a number of 'God's' in it. This is absolutely ridiculous! It is like Alice in Wonderland saying 'shit', or Bertie Wooster saying 'bugger'! I really cannot understand the mentality which carefully builds up an amusing, ingenious and enjoyable show and then puts in language which totally destroys the effect which has been created. Please excise all bad language from all future 'Goodies', and, if there is any in the shows which you have already done, please remove it, where necessary, leaving a jump-cut where the excision has been made. Better a jump-cut which will hardly be noticed than the bad language which undoubtedly will!*

Tim struggles with a 'snake' on location in Ealing.

'He thought it tarnished the show,' says Tim. 'Bill serves a guinea pig a meal. All I said was "Bloody hell!" but that was frowned upon. For the remake I had to say "Ruddy hell!" instead. You may notice me overemphasise the line, but it was deliberate. I wanted to make the point about how bloody stupid it was!'

As part of the rules for Montreux, the entered programme had to have been screened in the country of origin within the previous six months. As this was a re-worked version of the original show, it was hastily allotted a time in the schedule before the Montreux winner was announced at the end of May. 'Kitten Kong' came second to Austria's 'Lodynski's Flohmarket Company' and received the Silver Rose. In 'The New Office', the first episode of the third series, Tim is seen watering the prize and desperately painting it gold!

But the BBC was chuffed. The production office and the Goodies themselves received a letter from the Board of Governors: 'To express the very great pleasure which they felt on learning of the award of the Silver Rose of Montreux to *The Goodies*. The series is one which has given many of us great delight and it is a considerable satisfaction that it has now received this particularly striking recognition.'

I'M SORRY I HAVEN'T A CLUE

The day after the revised edition of 'Kitten Kong' was first broadcast, Tim, Graeme and Bill joined forces with *I'm Sorry I'll Read That Again* alumnus John Cleese and Jo Kendall for this 'antidote to panel games'.

First mentioned in September 1971 and originally entitled *I'm Sorry, They're At It Again*, the pilot show was recorded at the Playhouse on 16 November. A series was broadcast on Radio 4 from April to July 1972. Creator Graeme explains: 'Basically it was an attempt to recreate the fun of *I'm Sorry I'll Read That Again*, but without the BBC having to pay us for writing the script! The BBC was delighted with that concept. It was also attractive, for me at any rate, to simply record a programme. Not to have to sit down and write a script was lovely. It was as cold-blooded as that.'

Bill concurs: 'It was Graeme's bloody stupid idea! "Hey, I've got a great idea, BBC," he would have said. "We'll come along, do half an hour of comedy for you and you don't have to pay us to write it!" I said, "Graeme, that's a very bad idea." The BBC loved it, of course!'

Graeme recalls that he 'suggested the idea to David Hatch who, as well as being in the shows, had also produced the last *I'm Sorry I'll Read That Again*s, and we recorded the pilot. Pretty much everything was ad-libbed in that first series. That was a mistake. The audience like to see you being put on the spot and sweat a bit, but it is almost impossible to record half an hour of comedy without a script. I say almost impossible, because we were able to do it somehow.'

In a March 1972 BBC memo from Mary Herring of the copyright department to agent Brian Codd it was revealed that:

We hope to broadcast thirteen (twelve and the pilot) radio programmes ... and David Hatch tells me that

at the moment we think that Graeme Garden will take part in twelve programmes and Bill Oddie in ten. After a long discussion with Graeme Garden (the original deviser of the panel game) it has been agreed by all the participants that the best way to make the game work really properly is for all the contestants on each individual show to contribute to the devising of that particular programme. The contestants will be

responsible for devising the rounds, the subjects to be chosen for calypsos etc. and certain small items of script. We think the amount of work involved will justify, as it did on the pilot, the total fee of £40 and we suggest that it should be split between the four contestants as being the fairest way of dealing with this aspect of the programme.

The pressure wasn't to everybody's taste: 'Humphrey Lyttelton and Barry Cryer were the chairmen, doing alternate shows I think,' says Bill. 'But their job was fairly straightforward. As long as they remembered who we were they were pretty safe. For the rest of us it was a bloody nightmare. Thank God it wasn't live! It's the only show I just gave up on. In those days they tried to do several shows in one day and it was just agony. And, of course, all the best bits were the bits you had worked on in the pub before going on because they were all written, but you weren't paid for them! But it literally made me ill. I didn't enjoy it at all. In fact I was frequently sick before we went out to face the audience. And, as often as not, I was sick with the relief of getting it over with after we came off!'

The definitive line-up for *ISIHAC*. As Humphrey Lyttelton lovingly described them, 'a veritable "who's that" of British comedy.' They reigned from 1974 until Willie Rushton's untimely death in 1996.

A COLLECTION OF GOODIES

First broadcast: Sunday, 24 September 1972, 8.15 p.m.

Some more of the outrageous exploits of the Goodies.

Engelbert with the Young Generation had inspired Duncan Wood (Head of BBC Comedy, Light Entertainment, Television) to put together what was internally referred to as a 'Goodies Compilation'. As early as February 1972, when the Engelbert series was still in transmission, Wood wrote that: 'BBC2 has requested a special compilation of *The Goodies*, which is tentatively scheduled for transmission in early June. This programme would comprise selections from the existing new short film pieces made specifically for the Engelbert Humperdinck Show, linked by *The Goodies* team, and with new opening and closing title sequences.' Initial correspondence requested that 'The three Goodies … write and perform the new linking material – approximate total duration four or five minutes. The three Goodies to write and appear in new opening and closing film title sequences – total approximate duration one minute.'

Moreover, in April, Wood commissioned thirteen more episodes of *The Goodies*: 'I am anxious to get these thirteen shows contracted as soon as possible, since they

constitute a major part of our BBC2 output in 1973. These thirteen episodes will be broken down into two series – the first being of seven programmes and the second of six.' Contracts were duly signed on 8 May 1972.

Before signing up for the third series, the Goodies had recorded new links for the compilation special. Four minutes of material, written by Tim, was all that was needed to string together Jim Franklin's 16mm filmed inserts from shows seven, eight, ten, eleven and thirteen. The Goodies look after babies on Good Deed Day, work out in a gymnasium, make their West End debut on the streets *outside* the

'Every time you hear a train go by with "Daa-Daa" it starts *The Goodies* theme song! I should be on a royalty! But I was very aware that comedy music had all been tuba or bassoon. I hated all that stuff and wanted to move completely away from that for *The Goodies*.' Bill.

Despite wearing Arthur Mullard's suit Engelbert can't compete with the Goodies' muscles, courtesy of the BBC props department.

major theatres, steal a plum pudding (originally in lieu of Humperdinck's unpaid account) with Linda Regan as one of several Cinderellas, and perform as Pan's Grannies.

Jim admits that the team's natural reliance on silent comedy techniques 'were often augmented by the Visual Effects department's skills in specialist set-making, models, special props, explosions, dummies etc. Using silent film techniques also meant that the camera had to be run at many other speeds rather than the standard twenty-five frames per second.' Moreover, 'the "locked-off" camera could reveal items that could physically

never have happened in reality,' continues Jim. 'I suppose we were the only people in the BBC at that time employing techniques that were fifty years out of date!'

The twenty-five-minute compilation finally surfaced in September. Because of its cut and paste nature, the show was affectionately referred to as the 'Special Tax Edition' and, with a summer repeat of series two on BBC1, proved a useful overture to the new programmes.

CHRISTMAS NIGHT WITH THE STARS

First broadcast: Christmas Day 1972, 6.55 p.m.

The centrepiece of BBC1's Christmas schedule, this eighty-minute light entertainment and variety package was fronted by Ronnie Barker and Ronnie Corbett, who had just recently officially teamed up as *The Two Ronnies* for the BBC. With preproduction for the third series in full swing, the Goodies were commissioned to produce a five- to six-minute filmed contribution. Having started filming for the third series on 2 October, their script for the Christmas excerpt, 'The Goodies Travelling Instant Five-Minute Christmas', was accepted on 15 November. Within the next three days, the team had filmed it in the backstreets of Acton. With a poverty-stricken Tiny Tim (Paul Ellison) as its focus, the team conjure up such seasonal treats as double-quick carol singers, turkey-eating fairies and even Tim's Queen's Speech. Bill, as

Happy Christmas! The Goodies tug their forelocks to Paul Ellison's petulant urchin.

Stephen Fry and Hugh Laurie resurrected this format for

Fry and Laurie's Christmas Night With the Stars in 1994,

and a slice of vintage seasonal *Goodies* was included.

Bill looks amused as a swarm of Christmas fairies devour the turkey.

Santa Claus, chases the decorative Fairy Show Girl (Denise Distel). And a mini-pantomime sees Graeme as Buttons and Tim as Cinderella. Jim Franklin produced and directed the Goodies segment, while the rest of the show was put together by Michael Hurll and Terry Hughes. The scene was transferred from film to tape on 21 December, straight after the recording of 'That Old Black Magic' in studio TC4, and inserted into the master for broadcast on Christmas Day. Contributions from *Dad's Army*, *The Liver Birds*, Cilla Black, Lulu, Mike Yarwood and the Young Generation were also included.

It's Anything You Want it to Be. A Record or an O.B.E...

CRICKLEWOOD CAPERS

Although a successful comedy writer and performer, Bill's chief interest was still music. With co-composer Michael Gibbs, he had given the Goodies a unique sound. On 8 November 1972, the new title music for *The Goodies* was recorded. Conducted by Gibbs, the musicians consisted of Gary Boyle and Mike Morgan on guitar, Darrel Runswick on bass guitar, John Marshall on drums and Dave MacRae 'as ever on keyboard, and me on everything else,' remembers Bill. 'I used to play the kazoo or anything.'

'I knew exactly what I didn't want to do,' he continues. 'I didn't want that typical comedy music that accompanied every old comedy film I saw on television. I wanted to move away from the "wha-wha-wha" horns and give it a more contemporary feel. We used to have some fantastic sessions with

We Make It Happen Here

really good musicians just sitting in and jamming. I would tell them, "Look, this is going to go over some silly stuff of us running around and chasing a giant kitten or something and no one is going to listen to it and no one is going to care!" But it really worked. We recorded hours and hours of material and it gave *The Goodies* … something.'

Bill had tirelessly churned out over 140 comedy songs for *I'm Sorry I'll Read That Again* and would often resurrect them for *The Goodies*. In 1967, he had released an album of them, *Distinctly Oddie*, on Polydor Records. With the huge success of *The Goodies* and the importance of Bill's music to the show, it was a natural move for the team into recording stars. 'Or, at the very least, me,' chuckles Bill. 'I would love to thank Tim and Graeme for their contribution, but I simply can't! They were in the studio, of course, and, God help us, Tim and Graeme sing lead on some of the more eccentric numbers but, truth be told, I remember the lonely nights I spent replacing their backing vocals by double-tracking myself. Then I had to put my voice through a harmoniser so that they wouldn't recognise it was me and get all upset and sulky. "Yes, of course that is you singing in perfect thirds!" I lied.'

The first venture was a single release for Bill's rock arrangement of the traditional anthem 'All Things Bright and Beautiful', a version of which would be heard during a burst from the one-man band in 'The Goodies and the Beanstalk'. It was backed by Bill's composition 'Winter Sportsman', which was sung by the composer in the February 1973 *Goodies* episode 'Winter Olympics', but on vinyl by Tim – 'either that or there's something dreadfully wrong with my voice!' says Bill.

Although the single didn't trouble the British charts, Decca were confident enough to release the album from which the single came in January 1973.

What big teeth! Bill in 'The Stone Age'.

Graeme as Groucho Marx in 'The Goodies and the Beanstalk'.

THE GOODIES ANNUAL 1974

Reassuringly aimed at the 'kid's programme' audience, the Goodies had become comic-strip heroes in 1972 when they were featured in the pages of *Cor!!* comic and the 1973 *Cor!! Annual.* Indeed, Bill had relinquished his usual *Beano* in favour of *Cor!!* in the episodes 'For Those in Peril on the Sea' and 'Camelot'. Copyrighted exclusively to Tim, Graeme and Bill, the comic strips form a large part of the official *Goodies Annual*, although 'none of us had anything to do with the design or stories', explains Graeme. 'But we were very happy with the results.' Packed with corny gags, these sit alongside other features including 'The Greatest Story Ever Told, or how did three silly people like the Goodies ever get their own show on television' and 'All Together Now', depicting the Goodies in the studio recording their first album. There's a game inspired by 'Kitten Kong' (The Search for Mighty Mice!), three pen and ink sketches forming 'The Goodies by the Goodies' and even a comic-strip commercial break advertising the Common Market Burger from Heimz!

The Goodies gleefully plug the annual, *Cor!!* Comic and Goodies T-Shirts.

THE GOODIES SING SONGS FROM THE GOODIES

It was a joke come true,' says Bill. 'A guy I used to play charity football with, Miki Antony, who was a record producer, quite rightly saw an opportunity there, and since the music was on the show, it was self-promoting.' At least no unsuspecting record buyer could complain that the title was misleading for, indeed, here were the Goodies singing songs that had either featured on the show or that would soon feature in the upcoming third series. There was 'Stuff That Gibbon' from 'That Old Black Magic', 'Taking Me Back' from 'Camelot', 'Ride My Pony' from 'Hunting Pink', 'Spacehopper' from series two's 'Charity Bounce' and, of course, the *Goodies* theme itself. However, the major inspiration for the record was the June 1973 special, 'Superstar', which allowed Bill to indulge in his rock-stardom fantasies and which would also showcase 'Mummy, I Don't Like My Meat'.

The only number on the album not penned by Bill was the unfinished ditty, 'The Sparrow Song', which runs throughout the selection. It momentarily becomes 'The Butterfly Song' before the team throw in the towel, and was written by Graeme. The song was also resurrected for the 'Superstar' episode, showcasing the Goodies as all-round entertainers with a name change to the Cherubs. It's so nice, in fact, that it's attributed to Tim!

'Take that gibbon by the hand listen to the rhythm of the band,

Slap him up and down upon the floor.

Tickle his feet and hear him giggle,

Then unzip him down the middle.

Give that gibbon a what he's hollowing for.'

The Goodies broke in to the pop market with the single, 'All Things Bright And Beautiful', and the album, *The Goodies Sing Songs From The Goodies*.

In the studio at Audio International and Theatre Projects Sound. Tim's performance is clearly not breaking the 'Singing & Dancing Not Allowed' policy!

Despite the thread of comic send-up running through the album, the record contains some of Bill's finest vocal performances. There is the plaintive 'Sunny Morning', which exposes the influence of Randy Newman (hinted at by Bill's original sleevenote: 'thanks Randy – oh what a give-away!'). The powerful vocal and John Mitchell's piano accompaniment make for an emotional track. 'Taking You Back' is vividly brought alive by Chris Spedding's relentless bass, John Marshall's drums and Gary Boyle on lead guitar, while 'Show Me the Way' wallows in the alto-sax solo of Pete Zorn. In fact, from Dave MacRae's keyboard to Bill's penny-whistle solo, the musicians are at the top of their game on the album.

Recorded at Audio International and Theatre Projects Sounds, Bill remains 'very proud of it, really. If nothing else it proved to me and the guys that the music stood up without all the silly running about.' And Bill insists the album has a message: 'Play your *Goodies* LP backwards and you will find out that Tim died thirty years ago … frequently … every night!'

Producer Miki Anthony coaxes Graeme. Altogether now: 'Flutter … flutter. Flutter … flutter.'

Series 3, Episode 1

THE NEW OFFICE

First broadcast: Sunday, 4 February 1973, 8.15 p.m.

Tim, Bill and Graeme have problems with an estate agent (Joe Melia) and his secretary Miss Lushboosie (Julie Desmond), build another office and have terrifying mechanical problems thereafter.

Jim Franklin took over the production reins and, for the 3–9 February 1973 edition of the *Radio Times*, *The Goodies* were awarded their first cover. Bill explained that they were changing their style, 'rather like Leonardo de Vinci changed his style a bit'.

Tim gave his opinion that 'a lot of people were very suspicious of *The Goodies* to start with. They wouldn't accept it was just a silly programme. True, each episode has a story, but basically we are trying to produce the funniest half-hour anyone has ever seen.'

Graeme's cockney charm, Bill's bearded baby and Tim's distraught mother – none of them can halt their relocation to a disused railway station, where they are put under siege attack by diggers.

'It was expensive,' remembers Bill, 'but right from the start we were conscious of the budget and how much certain jokes would cost. We were also technically aware of how a joke could be staged. We had an idea of how the effect could work and would actually write in suggestions in the script as to how the effect could be achieved. But we wouldn't put in an effect just for the sake of it. It had to have a point. In other words, it had to be funny, else it would just be a "so what?" moment. But the diggers were very funny and worked very well.'

Graeme reflects, 'We were working in television and the effects shots were done on film. By that rationale, anything was possible if the BBC were happy enough to pay for it! But often we would have to judge whether it was best to lose a £500 gag so we could afford two £250 gags instead!'

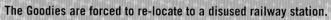
The Goodies are forced to re-locate to a disused railway station.

Tim suffering for his art as
his rear-end is attached
to a crane for a comic
stunt. Cameraman Stewart
A. Farnell is filming it for
posterity...or should that be
posterior?

Series 3, Episode 2

HUNTING PINK

First broadcast: Sunday, 11 February 1973, 8.15 p.m.

Bill and Graeme create hunting havoc; Tim gains an inheritance and loses his dignity.

Tim takes on a dual role as both his usual self and his manic Great Uncle Butcher, a typically grey-haired, insane member of the landed gentry obsessed with blood sports. Kitten Kong's owner, Graham Worswick, was once again on hand to provide animal participants, and it's kindly and radical Bill that rants on against fox-hunting. Indeed, Bill only gets the blood lust once he hits Tim! Aged character actor Erik Chitty, who had completed four years as Mr Smith in the hit London Weekend Television situation comedy *Please, Sir!* in 1971, put in a performance as the Tally Ho Towers family retainer, Baskerville.

The boys find more pleasure in a game of bloodless conkers; while Mad Great Uncle Butcher looks bemused on his Mad Cow mount!

'I was born in the saddle you know.' 'I was born ... in Sidcup.' 'I was born under a wandering star!'

Series 3, Episode 3

WINTER OLYMPICS

First broadcast: Sunday, 18 February 1973, 8.15 p.m.

The Minister of Sport (Peter Jones) persuades the Goodies to represent Britain in the Winter Olympics at the North Pole.

William Franklyn was originally cast but proved unavailable, and so was replaced by Jones. The glamour is provided by blonde bombshell Helli Louise who, like many of the *Goodies* girls, was represented by Barrie Stacey Promotions. She certainly proved hot stuff in the studio, although the session was not without its mishaps. 'I've always maintained that *The Goodies* was, physically, the most demanding work any actor could do,' claims Tim. 'We were getting hurt all of the time.' Certainly, during the secret training hut scene set in the coldest place in Britain – a holiday camp in Bognor on a Bank Holiday – Bill narrowly missed being bashed on the head by a fold-down bed that fell down a moment before cue.

Tim wasn't so fortunate. During the production of 'Kitten Kong', producer John Howard Davies had contacted the property master with a view to booking 'an operator and wires to suspend a trandem with three people on it'. The same device was needed again, but this time the wires were less than satisfactory. 'One of the wires broke while we were sat on the trandem and it really hurt me,' complains Tim. 'I was in agony. One of the stagehands actually fainted at the sight of my blood!'

The Accident and Industrial Disease Report from the studio recorded that:

The action consisted of a three-seater cycle with three riders being suspended in the Studio. The height from the bottom of the wheels to the floor of the studio was four feet. The cycle was suspended by three cables, supplied and rigged by Eric Dunning. The rear cable was so positioned that, during the action, it was in contact with the sharp edge of the underside of the rear cycle seat; it appeared from a superficial examination of the cycle that it had rubbed on the sharp edge until it had parted. This resulted in the cycle and its riders falling to the ground. Tim Brooke-Taylor grazed and bruised his back.

Two hours later at 5.50 p.m. the same prop, this time suspended by cables twice the thickness of the previous ones, slipped from the verticle [sic] causing the same artistes to overbalance. Tim Brooke-Taylor's hand was trapped between the hand brake and the handle bar as he was attempting to regain his balance.

Tim remembers 'vividly the BBC photographer John Smith dropping his camera to help me. A less caring photographer would probably have kept taking photographs, but not John. He was a nice chap. The most embarrassing thing for me was having to go to the nurse and explain how the accident happened: "… I was suspended in midair on a three-seater bike wearing flying goggles and holding a huge butterfly net while trying to attach a ray lamp from a butterfly in order to melt the polar ice cap".'

Brian Spiby, the Assistant Head of Artists' Contracts (Television), wrote to Tim concerning the 'report which has just reached me that you sustained bruises and grazed your back while recording … I hope to hear from you soon that you have completely recovered.'

Tim replied, 'The bruising and grazes on my back have quite recovered. The gash on my hand is quite deep, but soon I hope it will heal to its former glory. There should be no complications except, perhaps, a small, characterful scar.'

Series 3, Episode 4

THAT OLD BLACK MAGIC

First broadcast: Sunday, 25 February 1973, 8.15 p.m.

The Goodies meet a distressed witch, a seance is held, and Graeme has 'the power' – but is later possessed by the spirit of a gibbon. Time for a spine-chiller.

'Stuff That Gibbon', in a different version from *The Goodies* album, heightens the romp in this Hammer Horror-inspired episode which delights in the comic prowess of Patricia Hayes as Witch Hazel. 'I had been a fan of her's since the *Hancock's Half Hour* days,' says Tim and, indeed, the 'Come again another day' chant is a direct homage to her wily characterisation of Hancock's home help, Mrs Cavette. No one worked harder than Graeme, though. During the seance he runs through his stock collection of impressions: Eamonn Andrews, Walter Gabriel, Eddie Waring, he goes black-magic mad with the help of his shapely conjurer's assistant Betty (Patricia Gordino) and finally becomes a hippie sorcerer surrounded by semi-clad devil worshippers. Still, while it is Eddie Leroy who plays the shadow of David Frost, the voice of the devil is far more reassuring. It's Tim!

Tim needs you!

Series 3, Episode 5

FOR THOSE IN PERIL ON THE SEA

First broadcast: Sunday, 4 March 1973, 8.15 p.m.

The Goodies build a boat and search for a lost island; but find fish, chips and an old archenemy … the master of disguises.

Henry McGee returns as The Boss, alias Greek oil magnate Stavros Monopolopolous, alias Nasty Person, alias the Prince of Mischief. McGee was teamed once again with Norman Mitchell, who re-created his henchman, Gerald.

Among the rip-roaring adventure, the Goodies search for the lost island of Munga, not seen since the French exploded an H-bomb on it in 1965. There was a royal send-up, with Sheila Steafel recording the Queen's answer-phone message promising the children will be in attendance at the ship's launch. And the saucy girls are there: Wendy Bond, Diane Holt and Pip Wright as the native girls and Lynne Brotchie, Patricia Peters, Sally Avery and Sally Foulger as the Sailorettes. Finally, there's the usual serious message – that oil tankers are destroying the oceans.

'We're superior props,' said Bill. 'It wouldn't surprise me if the director's eventual idea is to replace us with dummies.'

However Jim Franklin understood the team very well, 'The Goodies, as a breed, were writer/performers. With good reason, they would be suspicious of any manipulation of their script by those who did not understand it. The programmes were enormously popular with young people, but they certainly were not a kids' programme. *The Goodies* resented BBC officials who wanted to transmit their programmes too early in the evening.'

'Wait a minute. Wait a minute. You remind me of some-

body.' 'Yea, me too.' 'Yea, hang on. It can't be!'

'It isn't!' 'It is!' 'Mummy!!'

WAY OUTWARD BOUND

First broadcast: Sunday, 11 March 1973, 8.15 p.m.

A 'Way Outward Bound' course is not what it seems and the Goodies are almost mutilated by a multitude of mini-monsters.

Failing to fulfil a commitment to round up children for the Duke of Glasgow Award Scheme, the Goodies are reluctant to turn down the opportunity of bagging £25 a head for each recruit. So they go juvenile themselves. Tim is kitted out in Little Lord Fauntleroy gear, Graeme appears as the saucy minx Miss Amazing Grace, while Bill is the school tearaway. But filming was no fun. The Accident and Industrial Disease Report for the filming details that, while on location in South Hill Park, North London:

> *William Oddie was engaged in a film sequence involving stretchable pigtails. This entailed a pair of tubes which were inserted into Mr Oddie's coat sleeves. The pigtails of the artist in front of him [Graeme] were inserted through the tubes and then out through the back of Mr Oddie's coat. As the artist in front of Mr Oddie ran away from him, so the pigtails were drawn through the tubes in Mr Oddie's coat, giving a stretching impression. As the knotted end of the pigtails came through the tubes, Mr Oddie's thumb became caught and was severely wrenched. He was asked if he would like to visit a local doctor but declined. He continued work, though uncomfortably.*

Bill was more uncomfortable about the guest stars. 'They were great,' he groans, 'but they got all the best lines again!' Indeed, Bill Fraser sizzles as Ex-Sergeant Major Ballcock. Having played the role of Sergeant Major Snudge for the Granada sitcom *The Army Game*

in 1957, Fraser would play the role opposite Alfie Bass's Bootsie until 1964. In 1974 he would reunite with Bass for a short-lived revival. Joan Sims, on the verge of shooting *Carry On Girls*, gives a touching performance that ranges from caring matron to world-dominating harridan. In a reference to 'Radio Goodies', Graeme sympathises with her dictatorial ambitions: 'I've even tried it myself!' he admits.

NORMAN MITCHELL

(1918-2001)

Prolific character actor who specialised in comic policemen, notably in *Doctor Who*: 'The Feast of Steven', Hammer Films' *Frankenstein and the Monster From Hell* and Agatha Christie's *Why Didn't They Ask Evans?* He was a staple of British television comedy with roles in *Doctor At Large*: 'It's the Rich Wot Gets the Pleasure', *Last of the Summer Wine*: 'Beware of the Oglethorpe', *Only When I Laugh*: 'Escape', *Yes, Minister*: 'Open Government', *Ripping Yarns*: 'The Testing of Eric Olthwaite' and *It Ain't Half Hot, Mum*: 'The Pay Off'. He chalked up four appearances in *The Goodies*, twice supporting the villainy of Henry McGee, and returning as the town crier in 'Goodies Rule – O.K' and as the boxing announcer in 'A Kick in the Arts'.

THE GOODIES FILE

Published by Weidenfeld and Nicholson in October 1974 and forming a collection of secret documents, letters and photographs compiled by the Goodies' charlady, Mrs Edna Tole, this is the first 'proper' *Goodies* book. An attempt to disgrace the team, 'Who are the Goodies?' puts the uninitiated in the picture with an identikit guide to the three team members. Tim's love questionnaire asks, 'So You Think You're Pretty Naughty?' while Bill's poem, 'Love It', reflects: 'There's a girl in 3C, with a wart on her knee, and a pimple upon her behind. I gave her 3p, and she showed it to me, don't you think that was awfully kind? P.S. Wonder what she'd do for a quid!' The team's pop success is charted in 'The Rise and Fall and Rise of the Goodies 1–12 Februarry

Promoting their first book proper while finding time to also endorse Tate & Lyle sugar.

1974', which suggested that the group had already disbanded: 'Rumours that Graeme Garden is going to go solo were described by the others as xxxxing ridiculous.' The book also includes a recreation of Pan's Nuns from 'Superstar' and the Mincing Monks for Bill's Super-Pope performance. Bill's other passion is reflected in the 'How to be a Bird-Watcher' section, but the most secret and damning file of all is 'The Case of the Royal Command'. Graeme would advertise the book by reading it (actually a pre-publication dummy cover) during the June studio recording of 'The Movies' and recalls, 'I think I had most to do with putting the books together, providing illustrations and helping with the design.'

FATHER CHRISTMAS DO NOT TOUCH ME

It was our first single under Bradley's Records,' recalls Bill, 'and most of our releases with them came from my Oddsocks Music Limited company.' Suddenly, an ascent up the British charts seemed a distinct possibility. This yuletide plea was released in November 1974, charting on 7 December and staying there for nine weeks. Its highest position was number 7, beaten to the top spot by that festive evergreen, 'Lonely This Christmas' by Mud.

Not everybody had the Christmas spirit, however. In January 1975, Mary Whitehouse wrote to the chairman of the BBC, Sir Michael Swann, complaining:

... about the record 'Do Not Touch Me Father Christmas' produced by The Goodies. It was included in the Tony Blackburn show at 10.15 a.m. on 18 December and also, I believe, in Top of the Pops. *The insinuations of the record were difficult, if not impossible, to miss and parents who are concerned that the idea of Father Christmas should be linked with sexual innuendo have written to me. The disc contains the line, 'You're a most immoral Santa Claus', so the inference is obvious. One mother told me of how her child had asked her, after hearing the record, 'What does immoral mean, Mummy?' and she justifiably asks, 'How do you answer that in relation to Father Christmas?' I would welcome your comments on this matter.*

Sir Michael replied:

I can assure you that this record was considered very carefully before it was played on Radio 1. As you will realise, the song is a variation of the old 'Sir Jasper' theme which has been popular in community singing for many years. The innuendo is, of course, there, but there is an absence of sexual explicitness and the continual mention of the girl 'standing beneath the mistletoe' surely suggests nothing more than kissing

and cuddling. In addition, it has to be borne in mind that the singers – The Goodies – are a well-known comedy team with a clean, if exuberant, image. Christmas always brings a crop of novelty records and this one was clearly popular with the public as it reached number seven in the charts. We received a number of requests for it and it was played in several programmes, although it was not in fact included in any programme directed specifically to children. This particular side of the record was also not featured on Top of the Pops. *Yours is the only complaint we have received about this record and, on balance, I believe we would have been wrong to ban it.*

Indeed, it was 'The Inbetweenies', the bop-a-long B-side, that won the most airtime, including two appearances on *Top of the Pops*. 'When we first went there, I remember thinking that the last thing the show needed was three sad old men, but once we got there, we realised that all the other acts were sad old men too, and that made us feel a lot better,' says Graeme.

Bill explains, 'We're talking Mud, Bay City Rollers, Gary Glitter and Neil Sedaka all introduced by a sad old paunchy DJ. We all felt quite young then, like New Kids on the Block!' The track reflected the lunacy of three thirty-something comics trying to be accepted by the young, and *The Goodies File* describes them as the Chelsea Pensioners of Pop. The joke was, of course, that they were accepted. For a glorious eighteen months, Bill would churn out hit after hit and the Goodies would find themselves performing songs in the most bizarre of situations. 'The Inbetweenies' started the trend when the team was invited to guest on the *Crackerjack* pantomime, Aladdin. Recording their contribution on 3 December, the show was broadcast on Christmas Eve 1974. They had also recorded 'It's A Gas!', a twenty-second jingle for Potterton Boilers and released commercially by Galbraith Music.

I'M SORRY I HAVEN'T A CLUE

Despite Bill's bouts of sickness before and after recording, he rejoined Tim and Graeme for the second run of episodes broadcast on Radio 4 between April and July 1972. John Cleese and Jo Kendall clearly lacked Bill's stomach. They dropped out of the team and allowed part-time series one chairman Barry Cryer to step into the breach. Humphrey Lyttleton was in the chair full time from this point on. As Graeme remembers, 'We were still doing the show completely off the cuff at this stage. It was very hard to be funny on every subject and you just couldn't compose an amusing calypso on the spot. If Bill couldn't do it then Tim and I certainly couldn't. So, eventually, we gave ourselves an hour or so before the recording to write ideas and pointers. We learned how to play the game properly. After thirty-odd years, Tim and I have just about got the hang of it!'

But written ideas and pointers came too late for Bill. 'I couldn't face the pressure any more so I said, "I've had enough!" There came an improvisation too far and I said, "No, sorry, fuck it ... I can't do this!" and left. I've never been back on it since!'

GOODIES SPECIAL: SUPERSTAR

First broadcast: Saturday, 7 July 1973, 9.50 p.m.

Bill gets a good agent and tries for stardom on *Top of the Pops*. Tim and Graeme change habits and get their tops popped.

The day after the last episode of series three was broadcast, the Goodies began filming the fourth series or, as it was considered at the time, the second batch of series three episodes. In the event, the BBC would break up the series into two separate six-episode runs. But what of the thirteenth commissioned show?

Heralded as 'The Goodies present "Superstar" – a special edition which takes the lid off the pop scene', the show was originally conceived as a regular episode. Always intended as the seventh episode of the third series, and in the studio exactly a week after the recording of 'Way Outward Bound' on 18 January 1973, it was given the 'special edition' honour by a nervous BBC who found the subject matter and comedy content too much for a show apparently aimed squarely at the family audience. It was Bill's ultimate wallow in the sex, drugs and sparkly suits of rock music. 'I had made some records with Gee Martin as producer and even did a Radio Luxembourg broadcast with a pre-stardom David Bowie with me singing some ridiculous Gene Pitneyesque ballad!' he says.

The Audience Research Department report of 30 July 1973 reflected that:

There was a decidedly mixed response to the Goodies' 'exposé' of the pop scene, although on balance it did not have the same appeal as their adventures in the previous series. About half the sample were clearly thoroughly entertained by the transformation of Bill Oddie into a pop idol (sequinned eyelids and all) and thought it a clever and amusing skit on the pop world – 'combined all the elements of the current scene – bi-sexuality, etc. – and really hit out', declared one, for instance. Several who usually enjoyed The Goodies, *however, did not care much for this particular one – the style was different, somehow (less 'mad', perhaps) and not nearly so funny, they felt – while others considered the programme quite stupid or were bored by the singing, which 'seemed to go on for ages'.*

The closing reinvention of Bill from Rock Bottom to Randy Pandy is reflected in the high-camp pretentiousness of the *Top of the Pops* St Augustine routine. A timely send-up of *Jesus Christ Superstar*, Bill is ably supported by singing nuns (Wanita Franklin and Ruby James), sexy dance troupe Pan's Nuns (Elaine Carr, Frances Pidgeon and Lynn Brotchie), and singing monks (Dick Hazel, Mike Rowlett, Jim Jackson, Mike Clarke, Mark Brown and Edgar Sleet, under chorus-master Fred Tomlinson). The studio audience, ideally young ladies who are over sixteen but under seventeen, provides Helli Louise with an illustrative walk-on role.

Barbara Mitchell, who played Bill's no-nonsense manageress Isabel Chintz, was considered 'full blooded' by the eighty-one viewers incorporated into the Audience Report, while for the majority, 'camera-work, costumes and make-up were also highly satisfactory, it seems, and the *Top of the Pops* sequence came over particularly well'.

Regular host, Ed Stewart, was originally signed up to appear, but he was eventually superseded by John Peel, who decided to play the part as Jimmy Saville instead. 'I had known John for years,' remembers Bill. 'I had worked on his label, Dandelion Records, in the 1960s. And of course Tim and Graeme beat him up in the Marquee Club after he gave 'The Funky Gibbon' a bad review! They were very naughty in those days. Graeme even punched Kenny Everett once!'

HENRY McGEE

(1929–2006)

Nicknamed 'SS' or 'Super Stooge' by Benny Hill, McGee was the star comic's perfect straight man for over twenty years. He was also beloved as the pedantic Mr Pugh opposite Charlie Drake in *The Worker* and memorable in a series of Sugar Puffs adverts with the Honey Monster. He claimed his proudest theatrical achievement was a two-week engagement in *The Mouse Trap*, thus giving him the shortest ever run in the longest ever run! As the villain in 'The Music Lovers' and 'For Those in Peril on the Sea', Graeme says of him, 'All the guests were good but Henry was very much our favourite. He was so good. A real comic baddie but never for a moment crossing the line into overacting.'

I'M SORRY I'LL READ THAT AGAIN

In a memo of 17 July 1973 producer David Hatch noted: 'It has now been agreed by the writers of ISIRTA [Graeme and Bill] that they will put pen to paper for a new series of eight programmes plus a Christmas Special (nine in all), recordings to start in early September. Various promises were made to the writers by Controllers and above, that any new series would be underwritten with a current repeat and a delayed repeat.'

'Everybody was free at the right time and we all wanted to do it again,' recalls Tim, 'so we did!' Broadcast on Radio 2 from 4 November until the day before Christmas Eve 1973, the eighth and final series saw a complete reunion of the classic team. John Cleese, who had left the *Monty Python* team – on television at least – had paired up with Les Dawson for his sketch series *Sez Les*. Initially reticent about returning to the radio show, loyalty finally won him over.

Still, he was apt to show his contempt for the overenthusiastic studio audience, as Graeme remembers. 'John got particularly annoyed. He wasn't overly pleased to be back doing the show again anyway, and if the audience got too vocal and gave us a huge laugh he would stare them out and shout, "Easy!". Bill and I started writing it into the scripts, in fact. It gave John this extra dimension. He despised the audience and, as often as not, he despised the script as well and that gave us great scope for comedy!'

Bill agreed with Cleese, at least on the issue of the audience. 'At first it was lovely to think they had got so fond of the show that the same people would turn up week after week. We even encouraged the booing of the corny jokes because it was fun … to begin with. Then it started getting out of hand. The audience would boo a good joke. They thought they had become part of the show and were waiting for the first opportunity to shout out and be heard. After a while we just felt like telling them all to shut up and go home!'

The series makes much of the team's various projects in the three years since the previous set of programmes. Cleese condemns the panel game he helped to launch as 'I'm Sorry I Don't Have a Script', while Tim's radio series, *Hello Cheeky*, is shamelessly sent up. Even his faithful old character, Lady Constance, fails to make her entrance because the creator of the character has forgotten how to do her voice! An emergency operation assures her resurrection at the close of the first episode.

'The Lady Constance de Coverlet character was an extension of the Lady Bracknell character I played in the *Cambridge Circus* send-up of Oscar Wilde,' remembers Tim. 'Dame Edith Evans, on whom it was based, came to the first night at the Lyric in the West End and was, apparently, the only person who didn't realise who I was impersonating. Kenneth Tynan in his review called my impersonation "blasphemous".'

Over the eight-programme run, Bill introduced his 'Terrapin Song', 'Sick Man Blues' and 'Cactus in My Y-Fronts' (all later added to the Goodies songbook) and the team presented 'The Colditz Story'. There's also the ultimate Victorian nightmare in 'Sherlock Holmes meets Jack the Ripper', Graeme's Eddie Waring hosts 'It's A Cock-Up' and the finals of the Miss United Prune competition are held.

As Bill explains, 'Radio comedy had always been a bit near the knuckle. I mean, *Round the Horne* was relentless. And so were we. We enjoyed it. We even put in some outrageous lines on purpose, knowing full well that the powers that be wouldn't notice but the audience would. Some gags would be crossed out but, as the years went on it got more and more relaxed. The BBC knew what the programme was all about and we were very well protected by our producer, David Hatch. As soon as one of "us" also became one of "them" we could get away with almost anything.'

Series 4, Episode 1

CAMELOT

First broadcast: Saturday, 1 December 1973, 8 p.m.

The Goodies save a semidetached castle, do battle with a dragon and duel with a devious destroyer from the Ministry.

During production for this batch of six episodes, the team was approached with regard to yet another series on 6 September. Officially contracted just six days later, the commission involved thirteen more episodes for a series internally referred to as 'The Goodies 1974'.

The script reflects the cult hysteria that surrounded the re-emergence of *I'm Sorry I Haven't A Clue*. Indeed, Graeme's 'olde' narration during this episode even embraces an *I'm Sorry ...* favourite, Spot the Dog, and the studio reaction suggests that they are fully aware of the reference. The corny-joke quota is also particularly high, with Tim's Jester dishing out groan-worthy gags, the literal coat of arms and the frozen fish-finger codpiece.

Alfie Bass guest-starred and 'he was a real pro', recalls Tim. 'He always made us laugh. While we were on location I remember him telling me that you could tell we were staying in a nice hotel because you could fart in your room and no one knocks on the wall!'

Right: Tim relishes a groan-worthy joke-a-thon.

Left: Alfie Bass stops the Goodies in their tracks in a barnstorming series debut.

Series 4, Episode 2

INVASION OF THE MOON CREATURES

First broadcast: Saturday, 8 December 1973, 8 p.m.

The Goodies in space crash-land on the moon, make a major discovery, cause havoc back on earth and give the Prime Minister palpitations.

Just four years after Neil Armstrong set foot on the moon, the Goodies boldly go where some other men have been before in an attempt to be the first British men in space. Tim and Bill soft-shoe shuffle their way through 'By the Light of the Silvery Earth', and the episode is steeped in science fiction and science fact. There's an appearance from Patrick Moore, a fleeting fly-by from Doctor Who's TARDIS and even a *Star Trek*-styled bunny chorus.

With Project Moon revolving around the influx of bunnies, Bill features in a direct parody of *The Quatermass Xperiment*. Infected by an alien virus, his removal of his glove to reveal fur stems from Richard Wordsworth's doomed space explorer in the 1954 Hammer Films release. Ultimately, the episode wanders into *A Clockwork Orange* territory. 'I'm sure the kids didn't know what the heck was going on,' chuckles Bill.

And there's an opportunity for a friendly dig at the opposition. Graeme panics at the thought of missing his favourite programme, tunes in to catch the opening credits of *Monty Python's Flying Circus*, realises he has missed Moira Anderson and turns off the set!

''Course we're not real rabbits! Oh, did I say that!!'

'It's wearing off isn't it...'

'We're still the sworn servants of Big Bunny!'

Series 4, Episode 3

HOSPITAL FOR HIRE

First broadcast: Saturday, 15 December 1973, 8.10 p.m.

The Goodies become doctors in the National Health Service; their methods of curing the nation's ills causes conflict with the Minister of Health (Harry H. Corbett).

Corbett, now fully back at the BBC as Harold Steptoe, and whose Christmas special would be broadcast the following week, seems to relish his Scottish Minister of Health role. Tim remembers he 'would have us in hysterics. He just went for it and there was something about those germs wriggling about. His performance of that always made me lose it during recording.'

And then there was Sooty. 'I recall the gag of the Minister blowing his nose on disposable Sooties, as a reference to the confusion between him and Harry Corbett, the magical puppeteer,' says Graeme. He then confirms, 'Yes, all medical students are so obsessed [with beer and nurses], or were in my day. This was

Alas poor Harry! A distinguished Shakespearean actor in his youth, Harry H. Corbett grabs a chance to break away from his familiar Steptoe role.

put to endless good use in our scripts for *Doctor in the House*.' And, indeed, the Thames sitcoms *Doctor At Large* and *Doctor In Charge* in the early 1970s. Graeme and Bill could be more subversive on the broader canvas of *The Goodies*.

Finally, the Goodies medical show trundles into town, with Graeme as the slick quack doctor with a wonder cure that has Egyptian mummies walking out of museums and the dead rising from the grave. Ultimately overworked and in agony having healed the world, the Goodies find that there are no doctors left to treat them. But with Dr Graeme Garden around surely this would never have happened? 'No, that reflected the truth,' says Bill. 'Graeme is a qualified doctor, but he was no bloody good during filming. He couldn't even look after himself.'

'I might have been a very good doctor,' said Graeme, 'but not a very happy one. It's nice when people I know who are good doctors come up and say what a good job you are doing making people laugh. It makes me feel very humble.'

Special Holiday Edition

THE GOODIES AND THE BEANSTALK

First broadcast: Monday, 24 December 1973, 5.15 p.m.

In this special holiday edition, the Goodies barter their most valuable possession for some beans and get more than they bargained for.

Unlike 'Superstar', this celebrated Christmas extravaganza was always intended as an extra programme outside of the regular series commission. In a memo to the copyright department's David Gower, producer Jim Franklin asked, 'Could you please commission Graeme Garden, Bill Oddie and Tim Brooke-Taylor to write a forty-five-minute film script for "The Goodies Special", to be transmitted at Christmas. Filming will take place from 24 September–19 October 1973.' The team was contracted for the special project in August.

Made entirely on film under the title 'The Goodies Christmas Special', the unit filmed in London, Weymouth and Dorchester. 'I remember when we were in Dorset,' says Tim, 'that a huge amount of people turned up to watch. The place was full of kids. They had been given the day off school to come down. The make-up

Toni Harris, Marcelle Samett, Bill and Graeme are prepared for action!

caravan was rocking because of the crowds. We were in a back room of a little pub and they had put boards up against the door to stop the crowds getting in. People were battering down doors to get to us in those days.'

The extra running time allows the team to add poignancy, with down-on-their-luck Goodies struggling to make ends meet. But even their attempts at street entertainment are undermined by the eccentric dancing of a policeman (Marty Swift). They are forced to sell their beloved trandem at market under the auctioning hammer of Robert Bridges. The usual fairy-tale elements are included. 'There's a moment when I came back with a tin of baked beans in exchange for the bike,' recalls Bill. 'Naturally the guys are angry and Tim says, "I'm going to enjoy this!" and tips the beans over my head. That was his revenge after all those beans-boy adverts Graeme and I had written for him!'

The resulting beanstalk romp features regular Goodies newsreader Corbet Woodall, saucy nudists (Jan Adair and Monika Ringwald), a bathing girl (Toni Harris) and even a Girl Guide Mistress (Marcelle Samett). Finally, the Goodies end up at the foot of Mount Everest – 'or a quarry on Portland Bill, as the BBC knew it', says Bill.

To give the show a Christmas feel, the essence of pantomime is distilled into a special presentation of *It's A Knockout* and, as per usual with *The Goodies*, when the original talent was available it was signed up. Both Arthur Ellis and Eddie Waring agreed to take part, 'and that was after years of me impersonating him', remembers Graeme. Waring clearly enjoys the experience and,

Broadcasting legend Eddie Waring happily sends himself up. While Tim dons a mop for his Harpo Marx tribute.

after a lengthy stint as *the* voice of BBC rugby broadcasting, is indulged in a closing 'touchdown' with the golden egg. Suitably, all the *Knockout* games are geared towards pantomime convention, with wallpapering, panto cows, a coconut-loping Man Friday (Earl Stephenson) and Sleeping Princesses (Patricia Gordino, Christina Palmer and Helen Bernat)

THE GOODIES AND
THE BEANSTALK CONTINUED

awaiting the kiss of their Princes. The German team (Brian Craven, Ian Munro and Nick Thompson-Hill) and the Italians (Andy Dempsey, Lawrence Ferdinard and Robert Watson) fail, allowing the Goodies to climb the beanstalk and meet the smallest giant ever (Alfie Bass).

Down 'n' Out Goodies take a break.

'I like the scenes on the mountain,' says Bill. 'There's lots of me looking down at the ground to stop myself laughing at the other two. I remember spending hours preparing the songs and the music and then the three of us going into the dubbing studio to put all these silly noises and sound effects over them! But there's a little feedback joke for the guitar players and the echo stuff works quite well. I remember Tim liking that a lot!'

Tim was less happy about some of the stunt work, though. 'We were still doing the most dangerous things and on location you seemed even more at risk than you were in the studio.'

'It's the waiting around on location that makes it appear more worrying,' according to Graeme. 'For example, sliding down a beanstalk. You get yourself into position and you're feeling happy about it. And you sit there and wait … and wait … and wait … and then somebody says, "That pole at the bottom there. We better be careful, he might catch his leg on that on the way down!" So that same somebody moves the pole. By which time you're wondering about the whole slide down the beanstalk. And then other people start talking about insurance and then somebody else ponders whether the stunt is safe in the windy conditions and within an hour you've gone from being happy about doing it to being absolutely nerve-wracked. I always felt safest when the dummies were doing the stunt!'

For Bill, though, 'The general rule was, if it wasn't uncomfortable it wasn't going to work!'

The actual exteriors for the castle were filmed outside the prison on Portland Bill although the fairy-tale domain spotted atop the mountain was a model. In fact, 'It was left out overnight and somebody nicked it,' says Graeme.

Once within the castle, the Goodies are memorably put through their paces with an oversized cup, an oversized

Helli Louise shows of her beautiful puppies!

Alfie Bass posing with a balloon ... for some reason!

cake and, ultimately, an oversized boot on the rampage. However, the best-remembered castle scene has the team singing Cole Porter's 'Who Wants To Be A Millionaire?' while paying homage to the Marx Brothers. Tim, Graeme and Bill recorded the number with the Michael Gibbs Group and the Dick Hazel Singers. It would prove an enjoyable interlude before the escape from the giant and those iconic dam-busting geese.

'Again, all that was quite dangerous,' says Bill. 'I remember Tim having to wear a metal protector under a wig when we dropped an egg on his head! They were bloody heavy those eggs, you know. It might have scrambled him!'

He continues, 'And I loved all the Hitchcock references to *The Birds*. I remember insisting on one particular shot when we are nervously looking around and the goose pops up menacingly into shot. People thought that was a bit too frightening, but we wanted it in. You had to pity the poor guy holding the goose though.'

The closing scene includes the last of the promised 'other surprise guests' as a burst of the 'Liberty Bell'

ushers in John Cleese in full *Monty Python* announcer outfit and a genie's hat. Instructed to 'push off' by Tim, Cleese retaliates with a barbed 'Kid's programme!'

'Our little dig at the BBC,' is how Bill describes it. 'I suppose the beanstalk was more of a kid's programme than what we usually did. But it was more like the Goodies' take on a kid's story, which is a very different thing. But it was crazy at the BBC. We had been quite satirical and on the edge, but suddenly they realised that kids were enjoying the show. They weren't our sole audience by any means. If anything I suppose we were that dreaded thing: the "family" show. Not that we were cosy, but we worked on several levels so the dads could get the saucy bits and the kids could laugh at Tim being beaten up. But once the BBC labelled us a kid's programme we were facing all sorts of problems about what we could and could not put in the show!'

Tim agrees: 'It became a bit of a curse. I always liked what Frank Muir said about us, that we were childlike rather than childish.'

Series 4, Episode 4

THE STONE AGE

First broadcast: Saturday, 29 December 1973, 8.05 p.m.

There's trouble with a tyrannosaurus rex, as Graeme's love of archaeology lands the Goodies in a subterranean predicament.

This was the first example of a recurring situation – just Tim, Graeme and Bill and a single set. 'We did several of those,' says Tim, 'and in many ways they are my favourites. We were forced to act rather than just be a human cartoon.'

'It usually happened at the end of the series,' comments Bill, 'when the budget had been spent on all the big effects and there was nothing left.'

'Though, to be fair, we planned it like that,' reflects Graeme. 'We knew we had to be a bit cleverer in our writing at the end of a series and work in one of those shows where it was just us and nothing else.'

Indeed, while the rest of the six-episode block was in studio during May and June 1973, this particular show wasn't recorded until November, thus making its simplicity a blessing. What's more, there is Bill's ventriloquist's dummy act to savour and a one-man-a-side football match between Bill's Chelsea and Tim's Derby County.

Keeping it simple: The Goodies face life inside a dinosaur's belly.

Series 4, Episode 5

GOODIES IN THE NICK

First broadcast: Saturday, 5 January 1974, 6.45 p.m.

Police Sergeant Shark (Jack Douglas) wants promotion, but he's scared of criminals. The Goodies rob a bank so that Shark can catch them; trouble is, they escape...

Douglas who, at the time of recording on 1 June 1973, was just about to start in the stage revue *Carry On London!*, retains traits of his Northern bumbler Alf Impititimus for his sweet and innocent policeman who, after twenty-five years in the force, has only two arrests to his name.

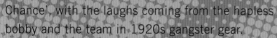

Although police corruption is hinted at, this is a far jollier romp than 'Give Police A Chance', with the laughs coming from the hapless bobby and the team in 1920s gangster gear.

Tim is the Marlon Brando-styled Goodiefather, while returning supporting actor Erik Chitty, from 'Hunting Pink', is the short-sighted witness Mr Dennison. Tommy Godfrey, from 'For Art's Sake', is the loud-mouthed barker at the court introducing legal characters Issy Bent and Justice Once!

Series 4, Episode 6

THE RACE

First broadcast: Saturday, 12 January 1974, 6.45 p.m.

The Goodies are in France, where they build a car and go racing at Le Mans.

In this episode *The Great Race*, *It's A Mad, Mad, Mad, Mad World* and *Those Magnificent Men in Their Flying Machines* are all rolled into one. Indeed, the fiendish Baron O'Beef (Bill Weston) radiates the grinning charm of Terry Thomas. There's even a moment of *Chitty Chitty Bang Bang*-inspired aeronautics, when Graeme adapts their roadworthy office and flies off into the sunset to a suitably French '*Fin*' finale.

'We shall beat these cocky foreigners.

Them and their garlic bicycles. We are best.

For we are British.'

G You Need a Helping Hand. O You'll Know We'll Understand.

THE YEAR OF THE GOODY

A fifth series of *The Goodies* had been on the cards since August 1973 when Duncan Wood wrote: 'Dear all, following our meeting, herewith, as promised, a proposed production schedule for thirteen more of *The Goodies* to be done in 1974.' Jim Franklin's suggestions were taken on board in that 'there should be a four-week period here instead of two weeks. Jim thinks that some of his lads will need a holiday period about here, and I would assume that this suggestion might be equally welcome to everybody else.' In a further memo of 24 September 1973, Wood declared, 'Now that terms have been agreed with the agents ... both for performance and copyright fees, would you please go ahead and formally contract them for thirteen programmes over the following schedule...'

O We'll be there to the end. Everyone needs a friend.

He went on to propose that the first seven shows be recorded by the end of July 1974, with the remaining six to be finished by the end of the year.

However, by June 1974, with just two programmes completed in the studio, industrial action at the BBC dictated that five shows be postponed due to lack of studio space. This resulted in the entire fifth series being held back for broadcast until early 1975, over a year since the end of the fourth series.

Despite the upheaval, the series saw several iconic additions and alterations to *The Goodies*. Firstly, Tim's Union Jack waistcoat was unveiled for the first time,

firmly establishing the character as the pro-royal, posh member of the team. The series also introduced a brand-new version of *The Goodies* theme tune.

And, perhaps most crucially of all, the series saw the team return to being broadcast at a later hour, a move that the Goodies themselves had been requesting 'because we were all fed up of being branded kids' entertainers', explains Bill. 'We begged the BBC to put us out at nine o'clock, which they eventually did. Then, of course, we got hundreds and hundreds of letters from kids complaining that we were going out after their bedtime and that they couldn't watch us any more!'

A water-logged Royal garden party in the Christmas special 'Goodies – Rule O.K'

Indeed, the Audience Research report for the first episode of the new series was issued on 26 February 1975 and revealed, 'There was plenty to enjoy in this "fast-moving" and "inventive" comedy. Some said they were delighted to have the series back and felt this first show was as "brilliant" and "hilarious" as ever. A few added that their children greatly enjoyed it – an earlier transmission time was occasionally requested.'

But Bill stands by the team's desire for a later slot. 'I don't think it bothered most kids. Thousands must have been staying up later then their bedtimes *and* telling their friends because our viewing figures went from three million to ten million. Suddenly we were big news!'

Tim agrees. 'It seemed to happen overnight, although we had been popular for three or four years. It was at that moment *The Goodies* seemed to become "socially acceptable" I suppose. We won the *Sun* award, with *Morecambe and Wise* coming second and *The Two Ronnies* third! Our records were selling in huge numbers, the books were bestsellers. It all happened in 1975!'

Asked during the Montreux promotional how all these strings to their bow made them feel, the group answered: 'Tired...' It was hardly surprising that when the series finally returned to BBC television, *The Goodies* received its second *Radio Times* cover for the 8–14 February 1975 issue.

'As performers, I think we really hit our stride at this stage,' believes Bill. 'Whenever I watch an episode back I'm always struck by just how damn good Tim and Graeme are and I'm not being soppy when I say that. I really do enjoy watching them. Graeme is such a good actor and he's one of the only people I know who can always keep a straight face no matter what madness is going on around him. That was in sharp contrast to Tim and I. I remember one time when Tim and I were giggling so much at each other during a recording that we had to be put into different studios and do it a line at a time and feed it through. I just have to think about Tim and I start laughing ... in the nicest possible way of course!'

SHEILA STEAFEL
(1939–)

A dependable actress with a talent for comedy, she appeared in sketches on *The Frost Report* and *The World of Beachcomber*, while enjoying regular work on Spike Milligan's *Q* shows and Kenny Everett's programmes. The voice of the Queen on *The Goodies*, she was first heard in 'For Those in Peril on the Sea' and she continued regally in 'Scatty Safari', 'The End' and 'Goodies Rule – O.K'. She was unavailable for 'Royal Command' and was replaced by Jill Clark. In the 1970s Steafel starred as the White Lady in Granada's *The Ghosts of Motley Hall*. In the 1980s she appeared in the Kenny Everett film, *Bloodbath at the House of Death*, and played the man-hating publisher, Miranda Shaw (pictured above, right), in Tim's sitcom, *You Must Be the Husband*.

THE MOVIES

First broadcast: Monday 10 February 1975, 9 p.m.

The Goodies buy a film studio, fire all the directors and make their own movies – the result is a stupendous Keystone-Coppered, Western, Roman epic. It's got everything … all at once!

Originally entitled 'The Goodies and the Movies' and recorded as the second episode of the series, as with most of the best shows, the fundamental peg which the team hang their visual gags and satirical barbs upon is a serious topic. Here it was the ever-deteriorating state of the British film industry and the pretentious elements that it was embracing from international cinema. In the wordy opening half of the episode, the Goodies take general swipes at the bastions of the industry and the

powerful figures behind it. Initially adopting the personas of Jewish film moguls with huge cigars and even bigger noses, the team lambasts the latest offerings from the most distinguished of film directors.

Graeme's pratfalling skill is fully utilised in 'L. Visconti's Death in Bognor'. Titled 'Slow Death in Bognor' in the draft script, it is a telling parody of the two-hour plus *Death in Venice*. Still fairly current at the time, having been released to great acclaim in 1971, Tim asserts that 'the joke is still current. It's still going. It's a very long film that lasts thirty years!'

Ken Russell fares equally badly in a mockery of his projects on the lives and works of great classical composers.

Tim maintains that the supposed

Sonny Day recreates Charlie Chaplin's legendary kick up the arse gag!

Tim and Melita Clarke, the only guest star credited, go for 'Epic' laughs.

Russell tribute to Spanish conductor and cellist Pablo Casals (Frank Chainey) is 'almost too close to the real thing to be funny'. Indeed, the surreal juxtaposition of images and frantic sexual undertones is pure Russell, while the stripteasing nun (Jennifer Somville) even had the power to shock Tim. 'It certainly fooled me, I thought it was going to be revealed to be a sexy girl. When it turned out to be a terrifying, white-faced, Italian clown, it was amazing. That was even more pretentious, which was just right, of course.' In the shooting script, Jim Franklin was to have taken the parody to breaking point, with the head of the cellist exploding. The draft script also featured a martial arts film, 'Kung Fu and Special Fried Rice', which saw a Chinese restaurant diner decapitating one of the waiters!

After the disappointing screenings, and having gathered together the finest film directors in the world, Tim takes on the mantle of a frustrated schoolteacher, reducing the likes of Fellini (Hugh Elton), Kubrick (Tony Boyd), Peckinpah

(Geoffrey Todd), Zeffirelli (Michael Webster) and Warhol (Richard Smith) to naughty schoolboys. It was one of the few scenes recorded in front of a live studio audience and 'it wasn't going very well', reflects Tim. 'I can hear myself getting in a panic because the audience are not laughing at it!'

Still, the laughs came when the Goodies get caught up in film production, firstly in a sequence with, as the script noted, Tim as a 'Mae West with poodles', Bill as the poor man's Richard Harris, with a 'huge Irish sweater and no shoes' and Graeme as a sequin-strewn effeminate.

As megaphone-wielding directors, the team produce the epic 'Macbeth meets Truffaut the Wonder Dog', which, as Bill says, is 'like funny movies you do with your family on Boxing Day'. These Macbeth scenes, filmed at Ealing Studios, were to have been much longer, with an aeroplane obliterating Bill's big speech and a desperate attempt to remove a hair from the camera lens only succeeding in making it even dirtier, ending up with a face being drawn in the grime.

THE MOVIES CONTINUED

Settling on making their own films, in the original script all three Goodies returned to the screening room in search of props for their respective productions. Bill's fixation with silent screen comedy saw him trying to hire the late Buster Keaton and Laurel and Hardy, only to be offered the 1960s comedy group The Monkees instead. It was a cynical embrace of comparisons with the team, which had become more marked following the Goodies' success in the pop world.

In the shooting script, Bill discovers the comic talent he wants in the archives, allowing for one of his favourite moments in the series. As the Goodies gather in front of the Feed and Livery Stables, the front of the building falls. It was a gag used by Keaton in *Steamboat Bill, Jr.* and Graeme recalls the danger of recreating the moment. 'In the original it's Buster who goes through the window, but all three of us went through the window and it was fairly scary trying to find the mark on the ground.'

Tim agrees that it was 'one of the most frightening things I've ever done … it was very heavy and would have killed us, but we all loved Buster Keaton and I think it was worth it … just!'

As Buster (Ernie Goodyer) dashes into the scene he stops,

White-faced Sonny Day, Dennis Hayward and John Cannon help Bill recreate 1920s Hollywood.

'I do love those old movies, don't you?

Aren't they good ah? Keaton. Chaplin.

Harry Langdon. Lavatory Meadows.'

'Lavatory Meadows?'

'He means W.C. Fields.'

Tim aids Graeme's Western movie.

ponders and notes down the joke. 'Hardly anybody notices it!' says Bill, 'but that was our little homage to Keaton. I liked the idea of us doing one of his great scenes and Keaton writing it down for his own use later. It was our little tribute to one of our comic heroes. And the other lookalikes are great as well: Laurel and Hardy [Dennis Hayward and John Cannon] and Charlie Chaplin [Sonny Day].'

These scenes were given extra clout thanks to the mythical Pinetree Studios being shot at Pinewood Studios in Buckinghamshire. The backlot had been left over from the village of Els Bels in *Carry On Abroad* and had been tarted up as a Western set. 'It was certainly beyond what our usual BBC budget could have afforded,' says Tim.

Graeme proudly remembers, 'We used all the original Hollywood techniques during filming. Nowadays it would all be done on computer, but we went back to basics, using a dummy horse for my ride into the town and a realistic backdrop for Bill's Harold Lloyd thrill scene.'

As for Bill: 'I loved the outfit I was given. I loved the look, it was like something The Band might have worn, and I loved the fact that we painted everything black and white in my bits, although I notice now that we didn't paint the custard pies, which was a bit remiss of us!'

So complicated was the conclusion that Graeme felt it necessary to make the storyboards three-dimensional. 'All our films get mixed up and we are running in and out of cinema scenes. I built a little model of the screening room and the screens and placed little dollies in the relevant places purely so we three would know where we were supposed to be at a certain time. I think it helped all of us to make some sense out of it.' The sequence paid tribute to another Keaton classic, *Sherlock Jr.*

Jim Franklin explained that, 'well over half of the programme was on film and was profusely storyboarded in order to be sure everybody knew what we were doing and how it was to be achieved. The visual effects element, always highly used, was particularly prevalent in this episode.'

'I think it was probably the most complicated thing we ever tried to do,' says Bill, 'and I'm amazed it worked so well. I watch it now and I'm quite impressed we thought of it!'

Bill on music for *The Goodies:* 'We would record great chunks of stuff. It was brilliant. We all got off on this great jam session. In a way we reverted to what those 1920s pianists were doing for silent movies in the cinema. Just improvising music which suited the mood of the image.'

A tribute to Buster Keaton. The boys recreate a dangerous stunt from *Steamboat Bill, Jr*.

CLOWN VIRUS

First broadcast: Monday, 17 February 1975, 9 p.m.

The Goodies dispose of the American Army's surplus soup; but it isn't actually soup, it's a virus that makes people behave like clowns.

That even includes the Prime Minister (Charles Adey-Gray) by the end, and the entire population has been infected by CV70 nerve-gas waste. Even the Goodies are infected, allowing Tim and Bill to indulge in some Italian-styled clowning.

With the blacked-up American troops finally defeated, they are rounded up by a finger-licking Southern Colonel (Ramsay Williams). Chief guest star, John Bluthal, picked up £230 for his performance as the larger-than-life General Charles M. Cheeseburger, and cannily supplemented his income by a further £30 by agreeing to 'warm up' the audience for the studio recording.

Tim invents Red Nose Day a decade early. General Cheeseburger (John Bluthal) hires the Goodies to dump his suspiciously toxic 'tomato soup'.

'Oh come on. It can't be tomato soup if it's green.'

'Perhaps it's pea.' 'It's certainly not soup!'

Series 5, Episode 3

CHUBBIE CHUMPS

First broadcast: Monday, 24 February 1975, 9 p.m.

Tim becomes terribly fat, then beautifully thin, Graeme takes over Radio 2 and Bill is squashed by a herd of fat ladies!

This show wallows in Tim's obsession with the housewife's favourite, Jimmy Young. Still, it was Terry Wogan's hugely successful Fight the Flab campaign that inspired the show. With Tim getting fit at The Lazy DJ Health Farm in a bid to win the Miss Housewife of the Year award, it's down to Graeme to urge the housewives of Britain to eat again!

Tim is still slim at the end and the clear winner, resulting in a Benny Hill-styled speeded-up chase. Michael Aspel returns, this time playing his *Goodies* parody self, Michael Aspirin.

Bill promotes his 1969 Decca single 'Jimmy Young'.

Series 5, Episode 4

WACKY WALES

First broadcast: Monday, 3 March 1975, 9 p.m.

The Goodies go to Wales, become a sensation in an eisteddfod, almost lose their heads to the 'Welsh druids' and beat Welsh internationals at rugby football.

The team had never before had the opportunity to be as topical as they could at this stage, with this episode, and the subsequent series five programmes being recorded in the studio just the Friday before they were broadcast on the following Monday. As Graeme explains, the tight schedule dictated that 'Jim [Franklin] did the edits himself – I don't think there would have been time to discuss any decisions in committee as it were.'

The industrial action at the BBC certainly affected the programme. Originally cast as the Puritanical Welsh barnstormer the Reverend Cllewellyn Cllewellyn Cllewellyn Cllewellyn of Llan Dlubber was *It Ain't Half Hot, Mum*'s Windsor Davies. He proved unavailable for the rescheduled studio date and was subsequently replaced by Jon Pertwee, in the immediate aftermath of his leaving *Doctor Who*. 'Jon was wonderful,' says Graeme, '"I can only do 'stage Welsh'," he announced, which was true, but he was very funny. He also introduced us to the ideas of "Freebies" or, as he called it, "Tut". Do a gig for someone who makes suitcases and get a couple of free cases out of it!'

Under his doom-laden gaze, the eisteddfod becomes the International Festival of Gloom, while tea and sandwiches are frowned upon and even lavatories are seen as 'temples of Beelzebub!' The show has every Welsh trick in the book, including an umbrella to protect against spittle when asking for directions to an ecclesiastical seven-a-side rugby match. And, in a bid to upset her once more, one of the players even mouths, 'Why don't you fuck off, bitch?' to Mary Whitehouse (Betty Morgan).

THE NEW GOODIES LP

Recorded in June and July 1975 for an October release, this was the first Bradley's Records album for the Goodies and collected together their recent hit singles alongside new tracks and one re-recorded number from the show itself: 'Walking the Line' from 'Bunfight at the O.K. Tearooms'. As the promotional material had it: 'The new Goodies album is more than funny, it's hilarious. And it's more than hilarious, it's musical too, in typical Goodies vein. It features their new double A-side single, "Nappy Love" and "Wild Thing", as well as their huge smash, "Funky Gibbon". We're launching it onto an unsuspecting public with a television campaign, heavy press advertising and a special display for your store.' According to the back cover, it was recorded 'almost live at the Cricklewood Rainbow', although in fact it was 'recorded and mixed at Olympic Studios, Barnes (about six miles from Cricklewood)'. Staying true to their comic roots and sending up the pop success they were enjoying, Bill is pictured on his knees in screaming rocker pose as Tim and Graeme unconvincingly accompany him on guitar. Their 'captive' audience is one nervous-looking cleaner bound and tied to her seat!

Actually on guitar were Alan Parker, Joe Moretti and Bernie Holland. Brian Odges and Tony Campo played bass, Clem Cattini, Tony Carr, Billy Rantim and Barry Morgan were on drums and Dave MacRae dominated on keyboards as usual. On backing vocals was the group Bones, comprising

Their first Bradleys **THE GOODIES**

The new Goodies album is more than funny, it's hilarious. And it's more than hilarious, it's musical too, in typical Goodies vein. It features their new double A side single, Nappy Love and Wild Thing, as well as their huge smash, Funky Gibbon. We're launching it onto an unsuspecting public with a television campaign, heavy press advertising, and a special display for your store.

will you be the Goodies next ca

Lead singer, composer and penny-whistle soloist, Bill.

Joy Yates, Jackie Sullivan and Sue Lynch.

'Nappy Love' had been released the previous month, charting on 27 September and staying in the charts for six weeks. Its highest position was number twenty-one. 'I played the tin-whistle solo on that,' reveals Bill proudly, 'and I hope everybody detects the Roland Kirk influence at work!' 'Wild Thing' was the first record that didn't come from within the Goodies songwriting unit but it remains one of Bill's most impressive, raucous rock performances. 'It was a tribute to the Jimi Hendrix version rather than the Troggs original,' says Bill. 'In actual fact, rumour has it that the vomit on which Jimi choked was actually induced by his hearing Tim's invitation to "Come on and hold me tight"!'

The album song sheet failed to reproduce the lyrics because, as Bill noted, 'Surely *everyone* knows the words of this one – anyway it's pointless trying to sing along 'cos you'll only hurt your throat…'

The single was produced by Miki Antony, as was the album. It was a cohesive, almost conceptual work, shifting

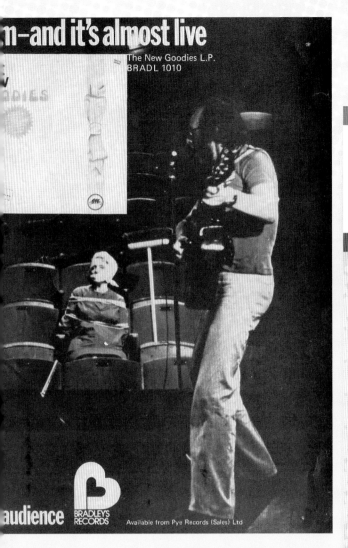

n–and it's almost live

The New Goodies L.P.
BRADL 1010

audience BRADLEY'S RECORDS Available from Pye Records (Sales) Ltd

Rocking Goodies in Bradley's Records'
advertising campaign.

MAKE A DAFT NOISE FOR CHRISTMAS

A Goodies Disco Special

THE GOODIES

Released NOV 28

SQUELCH ? PHUT OINK

"Make a daft noise for Christmas!"

c/w "The last chance dance"
BRAD 7533

YEEOW!

Stock now
Don't miss out!

BRADLEY'S RECORDS

Distributed by
PYE RECORD (SALES) LTD.
120-132 Western Road, Mitcham, Surrey.
Tel: 01-640 3344

the team from television comedians who resurrected
their incidental songs, to true pop performers with
an emphasis on comedy. Tracks like 'Cricklewood',
'Custard Pie', 'The Cricklewood Shakedown' and 'I'm a
Teapot' reflect the series, but in clear pop music terms.
The pitiful 'Please Let Us Play' and Graeme's languid
delivery of 'Good Ole Country Music' are standout
tracks, but it's 'Rock with a Policeman' that finds the
team at their peak. Bill's vocals are aggressive and raw,
while Graeme's mournful police commentary makes the
perfect contrast. It also serves as an effective close to
the first side as he asks us to 'please accompany me to
the flip side'!

With reference to 'Wild Thing', Bill commented,
'Does this perhaps point the direction of future Goodies
music? God help us ... and you.'

Released on Bradley's Records in November 1975,
this single entered the British charts on 13
December and stayed for six weeks. Its highest chart
position was at number 20. 'It was a good one for the
silly season, that,' says Bill. 'What can I say? It didn't do
anybody any harm did it? It was just me doing a silly Marc
Bolan sort of vocal and the other two making
daft noises!' The team performed it on *Blue Peter*
on 17 November 1975.

The B-side was 'The Last Chance Dance', featuring
Tim as a desperately lonely romantic on the dance floor.
Sending up the popularity of the BeeGees, this comic waltz
was credited as 'A Goodies Disco Special'.

Series 5, Episode 5

FRANKENFIDO
First broadcast: Monday, 10 March 1975, 9 p.m.

Graeme the dog breeder: fantastic new strains, chaos at Crufts, a scientific breakthrough and the creation of Frankenfido, the most amazing dog ever seen.

Graeme, gleefully slaving away in a disued church, produces the amazing Frankenfido by cutting and pasting celebrities. He uses Donny Osmond's teeth, the brain of Nicholas Parsons, the hair of Yul Brynner and one of Robin Day's legs. As Tim exclaims: 'You've been using people … and Donny Osmond!'
  Worse still, Graeme's nurse (Julie Mellon) feeds paint to the sheepdog in a wry comment on the Dulux Dog commercials. And Magnus Magnusson gamely plays himself in 'Mastermind'. He was approached by production assistant Peter Lovell who wrote: 'We would very much like you to appear as our *Mastermind* questionmaster in an episode of *The Goodies*. I have enclosed a copy of the script for you to consider (the relevant pages: 30–32). This will be recorded on Friday, 7 March 1975 in Studio 8, Television Centre, and we would need you for this day only, starting at approximately 11.30 a.m.'
  Bill, as 'Cuddly Scamp Hairy Legs of Cricklewood' appears with fellow contestants Hazel Nicholson, Tom O'Leary and Colin Francis, in one of the most memorable *Goodies* parodies of BBC television.

'We were on location with Tim, Bill and Graeme dressed as the six-legged dog, and a lady shuffled up to me and said, "Why don't you get yourself a man's job?"' Jim Franklin.

Series 5, Episode 6

SCATTY SAFARI
First broadcast: Monday, 17 March 1975, 9 p.m.

The Goodies run a safari park: they lose one star attraction and capture another, are beset by a plague and do a favour for Her Majesty.

The idea of The Goodies Star Safari Park seems like the ultimate reality show concept today, and the timelessness of many of the celebrities featured make this as fresh and funny as it was over thirty years ago.
  The Audience Research Department commented:

Three-quarters of reporting viewers thoroughly enjoyed this programme, which found The Goodies running a safari park comprising well-known personalities such as Liberace [Geoffrey Witherick] and Morecambe and Wise [Geoffrey Witherick and David Wilde]. To ardent Goodies fans, this episode displayed the usual 'zany', 'highly inventive' humour; 'the funniest show on television', 'so stupid, you have to laugh', 'wholesome, delicious fun', 'harmless enough for the whole family to view'. As well as the 'sly dig' at safari parks, the 'silly' views of well-known stars were 'hilarious' – they were 'all good sports, especially Tony Blackburn' – 'I never knew he had such a good running style'. There was some concern that the satire was 'a bit ruthless on Rolf Harris'; 'I hope he enjoyed it'.

Blackburn 'was happy to play himself', recalls Bill, 'and he did the whole Black Beauty thing really well.' In fact, he replaced Cliff Richard at the last minute. Dick Emery also makes a fleeting appearance as himself, while Marty Feldman appears courtesy of a three-second film extract from his sketch 'The Tourists Jungle' lifted from a BBC2

Preparing to unleash a star attraction from Down Under.

compilation programme. Continuity announcer David Willmott was also employed 'to obtain the typical BBC type voice with all the correct nuances'.

Rolf Harris was played in miniature form by Albert Wilkinson and by dozens of extras, notably Norman Rochester, Mike Mungaven and Terence Denville. The Audience Research report stated that: '"Sometimes we almost believe what we see!" Make-up and costumes were also commended, especially the Rolf Harrises – "they all looked alike".' Other celebrity doubles included Wayne Pritchett as David Frost, Brian Rix and Bernie Winters, John Cannon as Tommy Cooper and, intriguingly, Yvonne Paul as Danny la Rue.

It was originally intended that Wilfrid Brambell and Harry H. Corbett were to have reprised their roles from *Steptoe and Son* and a memo noted: 'Jim Franklin [was] to speak to their production office.' Sadly, it was not to be and Dave McMurray and Mike Travers played the sitcom totters instead. The *Liver Birds* stars Polly James and Nerys Hughes, plus Harry Secombe, were also

approached for a one-day shoot but declined.

The report continued that: 'With their exceptional talents, the three Goodies were "as good as ever". They "complement each other well" and are all "equally cast so that they share the limelight". "They really did seem to enjoy themselves in this week's episode."'

With The Goodies ridding England of the plague of Rolf Harrises, Tim is rewarded with marriage to Prince Charles. It was originally hoped that the prince would play himself in the episode and, for a short time, this seemed a distinct possibility. However, the Palace ultimately thought this inadvisable and stock footage was used instead. The decision didn't stop the cheeky end credit: 'The Goodies, By Appointment'. Indeed, the prince was keen to work with the trio in a short home-movie he had conceived. The film would have featured recently knighted subjects coming away from the prince with cuts and bruises. Graeme and Bill made the humour even more brutal with actual decapitation, but, again, royal advice left the film unmade.

THE FUNKY GIBBON

The ultimate Goodies pop hit, this Bradley's Records release from February 1975 entered the singles chart on 15 March and stayed for ten weeks. Its composer, Bill, admits that his songwriting was 'fuelled by no end of musical pretensions. Not to say pretentiousness. "The Funky Gibbon" was influenced by Miles Davis's fusion experiments, which were, in turn, based on the fragmented-licks approach of Sly and the Family Stone.' Moreover, once in the studio, Bill, the dedicated musician, would often take over. 'The guy on drums just wasn't getting the feel I wanted so I ended up playing his bit myself. The desired result was achieved by banging a rolled-up newspaper on the closed lid of the piano. I can listen to the track today and still detect the unmistakable sound of *Evening Standard* on Steinway!'

Perfectly scheduled to tie in with the broadcast of *The Goodies* on television, the unique hold-up in production of the fifth series allowed the team to reflect cheekily the chart progress of their latest single. With the Monday night broadcasts in the studio just the previous Friday, wall graffiti and Graeme's computer commented on the song. In 'Bunfight at the O.K. Tearooms', for example, a blackboard bears the legend: 'Buy Funky Gibbon'. 'Scatty Safari' includes the message 'Come on, it's Gibbon time' written on the wall, while another subliminal plug stated: 'Funky Gibbon – No. 4 + going up!'

Darüber lacht ganz England !

The Goodies,
die komischste Showgruppe
der Britischen Inseln (›Comedy
Award Winner 1974‹)
fordern zum Affentanz auf !

›The Funky Gibbon‹
(Hansa International 16 012)
bereits Top Ten in England
und auf dem Wege zur No.1 !

Do The Funky Gibbon !

Crazy ist in !

'The Funky Gibbon' conquered the world … and Cricklewood. Even the Germans fell under its spell. 'Unt, Unt, Unt…'

Alas, it was at number 4 in the charts that the single stalled, but the Goodies were tireless in their promotional appearances with two performances on *Top of the Pops* and further performances on *Lulu*, *Crackerjack*, *Blue Peter*, and the Bay City Rollers' pop showcase, *Shang-A-Lang*.

Graeme remembers the rock'n'roll commitments as 'acutely embarrassing. I never, for one minute, thought that I would appear on *Top of the Pops*. Why would I? Bill, of course, is a born rock performer. He was having a great time. Tim is totally fearless and will do anything in the name of comedy.

'We saw a monkey in a cage, doing a dance that could be the rage. It's not hard so let's all do, the Funky Gibbon ooh ooh ooh!'

Me? I felt a complete fool. I always felt a bit of a fraud, really. There was us, in our thirties, with a Top Ten hit record selling a lot of copies. And, for me at least, it was a sideline to what we were doing. It wasn't a big deal. But we would see these youngsters nervously waiting to perform after us on *Top of the Pops* or some such show. For these youngsters, the fact that their single had dropped three places was a life and death problem. We were having a good time and cruising past them up the charts. I did feel a bit guilty about that!'

But for Bill it was a dream come true. 'You know, everybody has said, "Oh he's a frustrated rock star!" Well, I wasn't frustrated, mate, I can tell you! I used to get my rocks off, as they say. And quite regularly in those days! Our records were in the charts. What's frustrating about that!' He does admit to one embarrassment, though. 'Looking back on some of the

old footage the only thing I see now is what a crap mimer I was! I look like I'm singing a completely different song most of the time. Singing "Black Pudding Bertha" or something and Tim probably nudging me and saying, "Bill, it's 'The Funky Gibbon'!"

Still, the track had international appeal. 'If not a worldwide hit,' muses Bill, 'then it certainly enjoyed a few worldwide cover versions. There was a German version, I remember, and an Italian one. That one was hilarious. After the "Ooh-ooh-ooh. Put them all together and what have you got?" bit, instead of the gibbon gibberish and cornucopia of "Oohs" that we had, they just said "Ooh!" It lost a bit in translation!'

The B-side was 'Sick Man Blues', Bill's brief, but potent, anthem of American rhythm and blues that was inspired by 'the way Tim sang it! That always made me feel sick!'

THE GOODIES BOOK OF CRIMINAL RECORDS

A fictional publication reflecting the legal battle between the Goodies and the publishers of *The Goodies File*, this proved another bestselling hit from Weidenfeld and Nicholson. Featuring praise from Marilyn Monroe, the Beatles, the Marx Brothers and even Adolf Hitler – 'I never stood a chance damn you, with respect' – the book had the Goodies campaigning for a better Britain, showcasing 'The Goodies Book of Art' and publishing 'The Tim Brooke-Taylor Song Book'. Classics ranged from 'Rule Britannia' ('Tim Brooke-Taylor, Brooke-Taylor We Love You') to 'See You Later Alligator' ('See You Later Tim Brooke-Taylor').

As Bill remembers, 'It was our year I suppose. We certainly had our fair share of comedy groupies. Comedy is the new rock'n'roll, they said. I think it was first termed for the Newman and Baddiel tours, but we did it first! The number of people who turned out to see us used to scare me, to be honest. And this wasn't for a pop concert. It used to happen on book-signing tours! We were in Manchester at the Arndale Centre and there were so many people there that the police had to go out and control the crowd. I had never experienced it before, but it really was that whole thing of the police saying, "I'm sorry, but we can't be responsible for your safety!" And this was for a book signing! We had become like a rock group, which is what I had always wanted us to become really. It was Goodiemania, I suppose!'

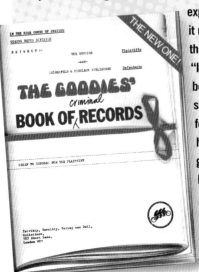

Series 5, Episode 7

KUNG FU KAPERS

First broadcast: Monday, 24 March 1975, 9 p.m.

Tim and Graeme try 'Kung Fu', Bill becomes master of the Lancastrian martial art of 'Ecky Thump', and black puddings fly.

Bill remembers this episode fondly. 'That show in particular gave me a great sense of pride. It sounds awfully pretentious of me to say so, but we really did love making the jobs of the people at the BBC a little bit more interesting. If nothing else *The Goodies* provided great job satisfaction. In those days ... and probably still today, although I haven't done any light entertainment stuff for years ... an awful lot of television production was so boring for the make-up department and the special-effects department and the others. They never got to do anything interesting and we loved coming up with things to give those departments something to really get their teeth into. We said, "We want a big flat cap," and the guy from the wardrobe department would come in with this cap about an inch bigger than usual. We would smile at each other and then at him and say, "No, we want a *big* flat cap!" He would keep on coming back with a cap getting bigger and bigger and bigger and finally they would come in with this huge cap saying, "Well, I think this is really stupid!" "That's the one!" I know

'Does not the gorilla have a fearsome jaw and yet he eats no meat?'

'Don't come the Mabel Lucie Attwell with us!'

The Grand Masters of Ecky Thump with black puddings set to stun!

they liked getting the opportunity to work on shows that really stretched them.'

With the current craze for martial arts films and the David Carradine *Kung Fu* television series, 'We added elements of Einstein cinema into the mix,' says Tim.

'We were all from the North Country and proud of it!' says Bill, before correcting himself. 'Well, I wasn't so proud of it. I couldn't wait to get away from the place, actually. But we certainly all had our memories and thoughts and prejudices about the North which were ripe for the show. I love the little film we did of me making the journey to the Mystic East [a fish shop run by Yvonne Ball] all backed with a mystic panpipe version of Gracie Fields's "Wish Me Luck As You Wave Me Goodbye". It was all great satirical stuff in those days!'

Vernon Drake was cast as Prime Minister Harold Wilson while William F. Sully played the Grand Master; 'and 'ee, he was grand!'

So successful was the show that one fan, Alex Mitchell, literally died laughing. The newspaper headline read: 'Man of Fun Dies Laughing'. 'We felt awful,' says Tim.

'In fact, we thought we were going to be sued by the family!' says Bill.

'But we received a lovely letter from his widow,' reveals Graeme, 'thanking us for making her husband's last minutes so enjoyable.'

'He had been laughing through the whole show,' says Bill, 'but it was the moment when Tim is dressed as a Scotsman with a huge set of bagpipes that did it. It's comedy so funny it can kill you. So be warned!'

Series 5, Episode 8

LIGHTHOUSE KEEPING LOONIES

First broadcast: Monday, 31 March 1975, 7.05 p.m

The lighthouse-keeping Goodies lose their light in a fog, strike oil in a gale, light a match and go into orbit!

Having misread a situations vacant advertisement in the newspaper, the Goodies discover that 'a little light housekeeping' is, in fact, a little lighthouse keeping. Bill is quickly on the verge of insanity with everything being round and recalls, 'There's nothing like a good row. Graeme and I used to write some good rows. Mainly for me and Tim!'

Graeme's playing of 'A Walk in the Black Forest' echoes back to 'Radio Goodies' at the end of 1970, but clearly some in the studio appreciated the joke. 'Our audiences were always very quick,' he maintains.

'But,' says Bill, 'the main thing I remember is that apart from the odd effects shot, everything was done in the studio. As a result of that we went over time. In those days we were fighting the clock to finish by ten. If you weren't finished by dead on ten o'clock the plugs were pulled. We went over time and we had to finish it another day.'

Indeed, the scenes involving Tim rocking back and forth in the bathroom and Bill and Graeme struggling to keep the lighthouse under control in space, were not recorded until 28 March 1975, a full month after the bulk of the episode.

Roman larks on location are enlivened by a visit from the Brooke-Taylor and Oddie families.

Series 5, Episode 9

ROME ANTICS

First broadcast: Monday, 7 April 1975, 9 p.m.

It's AD55: Ancient British Goodies help a Roman Emperor, create a holiday paradise, and do battle with Altila's hordes. See how Rome was burned and who was fiddling.

Despite the setting, the initial caveman banter addresses Britain's failing might, the Common Market and immigration. Graeme, as the newly appointed entertainments manager, invents the Olympic Games, while there's a wealth of sing-along puns including 'There's No Place Like Rome', 'Roman in the Gloamin', 'Rome Cooking' and 'Keep Right on Till the End of the Woad'!

Still, it's guest star Roy Kinnear as Nero that leaves the biggest impression. 'He really enjoyed himself,' says Graeme. 'He wouldn't just eat the fruit, he would literally squeeze the juice over his face. He was brilliant.'

Tim agrees, saying, 'I had great affection for Roy, but what was frustrating about him was that he was such a generous person he would never do the same performance twice! Every rehearsal was different and on the show it was just luck if you got a good one or not. He always felt he was letting people down if he did something similar.'

Series 5, Episode 10

CUNNING STUNTS

First broadcast: Monday, 14 April 1975, 9 p.m.

Fleet Street Goodies in a whirl, fire poor Bill and hire a girl, a rich man laughs to see such fun, and Bill's fired again ... from a gun.

Tim may be clad in 1930s reporter gear but the heart of the episode is tabloid journalism and the reverse of sexual discrimination in the workplace. Reporter Bill is blind to the most sensational story because he's blind with love. The object of his desire is Muriel Makepiece (Tessa Wyatt) and 'there was absolutely no acting required there', smirks Bill. 'Tessa was not only lovely but particularly brilliant in that episode. We were all making cow eyes at her!'

With lovesick Bill out of the way, she takes control of the office and treats Tim and Graeme as sexy, teasing fillies. Although noting that the advert forbids 'scruffy, hairy, frustrated pop stars', Bill is determined to make her father, Sir Joshua (Roland MacLeod), laugh. Even if that means being the sole suicidal entrant for the Eurovision Raving Loony Contest!

JIM'LL FIX IT

The Goodies recorded a contribution to the children's programme on which Jimmy Saville tries 'to make your wildest dreams come true' on 23 July 1975.

BLACK PUDDING BERTHA
THE QUEEN OF NORTHERN SOUL

Bradley's Records' follow-up to 'The Funky Gibbon' entered the British charts on 21 June 1975 and stayed there for seven weeks. Failing to recapture the full success of its illustrious predecessor it did, however, reach a respectable number 19 in the British charts and reflected the popularity of the 'Kung Fu Kapers' broadcast just a few months earlier. In a later episode, 'Hype Pressure', Graeme despairs of Bill's recent lack of musical inspiration and reflects on the days when he used to be able to dash off nine or ten chartbusters at a time. As a tongue-in-cheek example, he cites the world-beating lyrics of 'By gum, shake your bum!'

The B-side is another Bill original, 'Panic!', which allows Tim to repeat the patriotic cowardice as seen at work in 'The End'.

Genius at work! Director and producer Jim Franklin gave The Goodies a unique visual style.

JIM FRANKLIN
(1934–)

As an editor at the BBC, he made a name for himself on *Points of View*, where he had amused host Robert Robinson by dubbing refined English accents over an excerpt from the American Western television series *Laramie*. Later he worked on the 1960s comedies *Not Only ... But Also* and *The Frost Report*. On the latter he edited footage in such a way as to give the impression Prime Minister Harold Wilson was dancing the hokey cokey with fellow Cabinet member George Brown. Franklin worked on *Broaden Your Mind* and, as such, was a natural to direct *The Goodies*. He also directed the first series of Michael Palin and Terry Jones's *Ripping Yarns* in 1975.

'We owe a huge amount to Jim Franklin, our eventual producer,' says Tim. 'I had worked with Jim as a film editor on *It's Marty* and Graeme and I were very grateful to his input into *Broaden Your Mind*. The BBC was very much a civil service at the time and if anyone was to receive more money they were promoted. Jim was a great editor and director, but he was promoted, eventually, to be executive producer, which was not his strength.

'One of Jim's greatest strengths, however, was to draw up elaborate storyboards for all the filming. For several days the production team (wardrobe, make-up, cameras and visual effects, etc.) would sit round a table with Jim and ourselves, painstakingly going through each shot and how each department could help the others. It was this diligence that allowed us to make expensive-looking shows at a reasonable price. We now consider Jim to be the Nick Park of his day; without him *The Goodies* would never have worked.'

THE GOLDEN ROSE

Every year the television companies of the world send their best entertainment programmes to Switzerland to compete for the Golden Rose of Montreux. In this documentary the Goodies take a lightning tour through the city of Montreux in festival week and sample some of the year's entries, which include their own: 'The Movies'.

It was announced as the BBC entry on 27 January 1975. As a result it was swapped with 'Clown Virus' as the opening episode of series five. The festival documentary was produced by Tony Staveacre. Graeme summed up the tongue-in-cheek feel of the report by explaining that 'we are entered. And we are going up to people and saying, "Do you like us?" and if they say

no, then we're very embarrassed.' In fact, they were destined to pick up their second Silver Rose, losing to the Italian entrant *Gatti e Fattacci*, a variety show translated as 'Deeds and Misdeeds'. Still, the coverage warranted a repeat of 'The Movies' and this thirty-five-minute documentary was broadcast in the ungodly BBC1 slot from 11.45 p.m. on 10 May. It features footage of the jury watching the Goodies' effort, Jim Franklin picking up the award and Tim explaining that visual comedy equals international appeal. Roy Curtis-Bramwell, assistant promotions manager at the BBC, wrote to Franklin: 'So pleased you made the Silver – would like to have been there to celebrate the event. Maybe next time!'

The team's second appearance at Montreux in a flyer pinned to Bill's notice board.

SOUTH AFRICA

First broadcast: Monday, 21 April 1975, 9 p.m.

The Goodies 'sell' South Africa and cause an irritation. Poor Bill becomes a 'little' man and suffers segregation.

'This was a very controversial programme,' says Bill, and indeed it was. Seemingly plagued with problems, it was originally to have been recorded in studio TC8 in June 1974, before industrial action saw the sessions for this – and four other shows in the series – deferred to later in the year. Somewhat ironically, it was recorded on Friday, 13 December 1974.

'The BBC were just on the brink of saying, "There is no way you can put this out!"' Bill continues, 'It came back to us that we were being too nasty about the white South African police force! We just couldn't believe it. For a time we were all convinced that the BBC had some sort of illegal link with South African gold smuggling or were funding the white-supremacy movement or something!'

Indeed, in April 1975, Bill had requested that an old John and Mary sketch from *I'm Sorry I'll Read That Again* not be used in a South African broadcast of 'Frank Muir Goes Into … Jealousy'.

'The problem was that very few people in England were that aware, or indeed that bothered, about the problems in South Africa,' reflects Graeme. 'I mean it hadn't been that long since the Sharpeville massacre when police had shot sixty-odd demonstrators, and here was the BBC saying that our jokes were too critical of the police! It was madness.'

In an unprecedented move, not only were certain elements of the location filming edited – notably a scene in the South African promotional film featuring Tim's blacked-up fun-seeker kissing a girl and leaving

black make-up on her face – but the BBC demanded the studio session be re-recorded.

'We had been so shocked by their initial reaction,' recalls Tim, 'that we were on the verge of going to the papers with this claim that the BBC were corrupt. Instead, when they asked us to do the show again, they said that the attack on the South African police wasn't the problem. They were more concerned about me being beaten up all the time! Although, as Bill said at the time, our audiences used to love seeing me beaten up!'

Bill maintains, 'I'm completely convinced that they didn't expect a programme like *The Goodies* to make a political point. In fact, I blame Philip Madoc!' Madoc, who later that year would play the Frankenstein-like Solon in *Doctor Who* ('The Brain of Morbius'), relishes the part of racist Police Chief Piet Spoorshoveller. 'He was excellent,' says Bill. 'One of the best guest performances we ever had. Because he was so good you can believe that he represents the entire South African police force.' Tellingly, it was the opening scenes, which see Madoc assign the Goodies the task of promoting South Africa in a good light, that were the chief concern.

'In the end we actually said, "So what is your problem? Have we touched a nerve? Do you have connections!" But everybody was saying, "No, no, not at all. It's just that you have a nice, jolly little show here. Don't go and spoil it!" The truth is we had always been tackling serious subjects on the show. Perhaps this time we didn't cover it up as well!' admits Bill.

Graeme considers that 'perhaps we were a bit naive trying to expose the regime in South Africa in what was perceived as a silly comedy show. But it was only us trying to tackle these issues. No one else seemed to question it.'

The studio material was re-recorded on 11 April, just over a week before the broadcast slot, by which time

White supremacy is nailed to the wall in Graeme's conceptual sketch.

Mind you, the broadcast version was no less violent. After all, Madoc threatens to kill Graeme almost on sight! 'The rest of the show was pretty much as we had originally recorded it,' comments Tim.

'We just took the situation to its natural, ludicrous conclusion,' says Graeme. 'The notion of "apart-height" made us laugh a lot. And the point of the show was that a discrimination against short people is just as silly as a discrimination against colour.'

Mindful that certain elements of the show may be considered racist themselves, Bill believes, 'the whole "Amos and Andy" voice that I put in is simply commenting on the outrageous stereotypes that had been accepted for so long. It's also great fun to do that voice! But the main aim was to highlight the stupidity of apartheid. I mean, at the end, the blacks have taken over England and we are treated as the inferior minority. We even had a black Queen [Moni Adejumo]!'

Not to mention a black Enoch Powell, memorably played by Oscar James.

'It's because we were a silly, popular show that we were able to get serious points across to an audience who probably would never have thought about these issues unless *The Goodies* slipped it in quietly,' reckons Tim. 'We were a comedy-coated pill if you like.'

'Still,' laments Graeme, 'after all that hard work at pinpointing the disgusting situation in South Africa and facing the same situation in England, we had a chance of ending with some dignity, but Tim ruined it!' Desperate to blend in with the new elite in England, the Goodies use boot polish to black-up and Tim delights in a hand-waving moment of minstrel performance as the show ends. 'He just couldn't resist it!' chuckles Graeme.

'the BBC had covered their backs a bit', remembers Bill. 'They explained that the real reason they wanted us to do it again was that there hadn't been enough jokes in the original version! So we re-wrote it and put in even more jokes against the South African police!'

The revised version of the script included more visual jokes – such as the segregated black and white keys on the piano – in replacement of a more aggressive stance from Madoc's character. Indeed, Graeme's handshake with the policeman made him drop to the floor in agony and enquire, 'You want us to advertise South Africa?' Madoc responded, 'Hit it right on the nose,' and prompted a guard to push Graeme. Finally, Madoc pleaded, 'We want a really good film to show how lovely it is out there. You know people tell a lot of wicked shameful lies about conditions in South Africa...' Turning to the thugs (Ian Munro and Paul Barton) he snarled, '. . . don't we?'

Series 5, Episode 12

BUNFIGHT AT THE O.K. TEAROOMS

First broadcast: Monday, 28 April 1975, 9 p.m.

Prospecting Goodies dig a seam and strike it rich with clotted cream. But greedy Graeme files the claim, then loses all in a poker game.

The Goodies Western is perhaps remembered for just one thing – the tomato-sauce dispenser gunfight! Filmed on the streets of St Just in Devon, it proved painful for determined sauce-slinger Graeme. 'Tim and Bill gleefully tell the story of the Bunfight fall. I'd always noticed that when falling on hard ground it was the bony bits that got bruised, and tender knees and elbows were a real nuisance for the rest of the filming, so I used to wear pads on my joints. However, I decided I needed to pad my spine as well, so I bought a special spinal protector as worn by jockeys and riders, and strapped myself into it. In the last shot I launched myself into the air, spun, spun a bit more, and came down flat on my face with a mouthful of gravel. How they laughed.'

'Graeme falling off a stuffed pit pony,' recalls Bill. 'It was sheer poetry!'

Music also plays a major part in the episode, with a restyled version of Bill's 'The Lawman' from his *Distinctly Oddie* album, a later *Goodies* release, 'Walking the Line', and Fred Tomlinson's piano rendition of 'I Come from Alabama', which fitted the style requested on the script for something 'not unlike *The Sting*', with Scott Joplin's ragtime music being all the rage again in the wake of the Robert Redford and Paul Newman film.

Studio fun during the Bunfight session on Friday, 18 April 1975.

'You'll never guess what I've just found in an old tin mine.' 'Gold?' 'No, old tins!'

GOODY LOCATIONS

The pool at the Chines Hotel, Bournemouth, was used for Tim's battle with a shark in 'South Africa' and the Ken Russell parody in 'The Movies'. The nearby streets were used for the mini police scenes for 'South Africa', while Barnsfield Heath saw Tim and Graeme's encounter with Bill and the jockeys. 'We were all staying at the hotel and it was very posh,' remembers Graeme. 'A lot of the residents didn't look very kindly on these loony types from London taking over the hotel and being silly all the time. Of course, for "South Africa" we had quite a lot of vertically challenged artistes. The bar seemed to be the domain of this crusty old Colonel type and one night there was this little voice saying, "Six gin and tonics, please." He looked round and couldn't see anybody!'

THE WORLD OF THE GOODIES

Naturally a tad envious of the pop chart success the Goodies were enjoying with Bradley's Records, Decca felt the time was right to cash in on their popularity and re-release the first *Goodies* album, *The Goodies Sing Songs from the Goodies*. 'The World of…' series had proved a popular umbrella collection for repackaging old discs, notably comic ones, including *The World of Kenneth Williams*, *The World of Pete 'n' Dud* and *The Crazy World of Marty Feldman*. *The World of the Goodies* was offered up to the gullible consumer in May 1975 and remains an essential item for the Goodies completist.

Series 5, Episode 13

THE END

First broadcast: Monday 5 May 1975, 9 p.m.

The Goodies' travelling office – quality, trim and neat – is lost to redevelopment and buried in concrete. Bill has lost his reason and Tim is close to tears, and that's the way they stay blocked in, for over seventy years!

The definitive one-set, three-Goodies episode and 'probably my favourite', says Tim. 'We hadn't any money for new costumes or sets so we set it in our office. We were able to do more verbal humour.' Bill agrees. 'I always enjoyed the ones where there was no film work at all. We had to act. What a challenge!'

Several references to the Goodies as a team were lost from the final programme. Years into the future, newscaster Corbet Woodall was to say, 'The programme that follows is a repeat of a repeat of some old rubbish that you've seen before.' That would have been a cue for the start of *The Goodies*! Graeme's blues singing was to have led into a full-cast performance of 'Sick Man Blues'. And when Graeme finds religion and explains that their situation 'is all part of *his* plan …

Cricklewood madness … and those underpants!

he who sees and plans all', Tim says, 'Oh, Billy Cotton Junior.'

Tim's model of a synagogue would have been compared to another powerful television man's potting shed: Lew Grade's. Another cut scene during this interplay had Tim explaining, 'I'm just making matches, that's all!' Graeme counters with, 'Anyway, it's your turn to clean the shoes!' Tim would sing, 'If I were a rich man ... biddy, biddy...' and Graeme would complain, 'You're not Jewish, you don't know the words.' When Graeme joined in with a 'biddy biddy' of his own, Tim would moan, 'You don't know the words either!' 'Well I'm not Jewish!' replied Graeme. But at least one television reference remained. Tim's mouse, Gilbert, was named after the Head of Comedy at the time, Jimmy!'

The relevant Audience Research report concluded that the viewers found the show 'as funny and original as ever', although some were alarmed to see 'this likeable trio indulging in some "unaccustomed vulgarity"', most 'had the warmest praise for three delightful and "marvellously funny" artists whose complementary personalities made them an unbeatable team'. It was 'the highlight of the viewing week'.

With the comedy distilled to its most basic level, Tim can show off his Union Jack underpants and mock Bill's name: 'Billoddie stupid!' Graeme can misspell his own name during dictation and bring life to the inanimate Gilbert. Bill can become the Black Muslim, Rastous Watermelon, and naively end up on the menu. An aged Tim and Graeme can indulge in some Teddy and Freddy banter while a youthful Bill merely sees his posters of Davids Essex and Cassidy grow long white beards!

It's a thirty-minute, real-time spy on three people desperate for food, complaining, arguing and getting drunk. 'Yes,' claims Bill, 'we invented *Big Brother*!'

CORBET WOODALL

(c.1935–1982)

The personification of *Goodies* newscasters was a real newscaster who started his career on *Town and Around*. Having been dismissed by the BBC in 1967 he carved out a freelance career as a newscaster actor in television shows like *The Troubleshooters* and films, including *Don't Just Lie There, Say Something* and *Carry On Emmannuelle*. His dulcet tones were heard in such classic sitcoms as *Steptoe and Son* ('The Desperate Hours'), *Whatever Happened to the Likely Lads?* ('No Hiding Place') and *Citizen Smith* ('Prisoners'), but it was *The Goodies* that made him a comic star.

'He wasn't a well man at all,' remembers Tim. Crippled by rheumatoid arthritis, 'he would walk around on crutches'. Indeed, his eleven appearances should have been more, but frequently his contract was marked 'artist ill' and he was replaced. 'But,' continues Tim, 'as soon as he got out in front of the audience he was a changed man. He rose from the dead and delivered every time.' A scene cut from 'The End' cast him as 'Corbet Woodall the Fourth' delivering the news on 23 June 2041.

A HOLIDAY SPECIAL GOODIES RULE - O.K

First broadcast: Sunday, 21 December 1975, 7.25 p.m.

Goodies triumph in the world of pop, helps put Britain on top. They sink a Queen and float the pound, then battle with a famous hound.

The most successful year in the history of *The Goodies* was capped when the BBC commissioned another 'forty-five-minute Christmas Goodies Special'. The delivery date for the script was agreed for 14 July 1975 and, as with the previous special, 'The Goodies and the Beanstalk', the programme was made entirely on film. It was so full of comic invention that it was decided to extend the running time to fifty minutes.

The result would be the team's masterwork.

And for a generation it would be the one with the Giant Dougal. 'He was full of about twenty stunt guys,' says Bill. 'Clearly we had learned our lesson since doing "Charity Bounce". This time we let the stunt guys do the stunt and it was them, in turn, who were shouting, "Oh shit", "Oh crap", "Oh bugger", because of the pain of the costume!'

But the bulk of the show reflects the Goodies standing as a pop sensation – or, at least, pop

Dougal is coming!

wannabes. Barry Cryer's newsreel announcement takes us back to Liverpool, 1961, and the sound of the Bootles: featuring Graeme as Don, Tim as Saul, Bill as drummer Bingo and a shop-dummy George! A performance of 'She Loves You' is greeted by a bit of stock footage of a bemused Paul McCartney, before three rockers in the audience pick up the discarded mop-top wigs and the rejected sheet music of 'Eleanor Rigby' by Graeme Garden and 'I Want To Hold Your Hand' by Tim Brooke-Taylor and Bill Oddie.

The 'before their time' failure continues with the Goodies as the Confirmed Bachelors and the Extremes. Even 1975's 'Nappy Love' fails. Down and out and greeting *Monty Python* Gumbies with 'All right, John! Eric!' success finally hits with a Wembley concert. Playing 'Wild Thing' to an audience entirely made up of policemen because security is so tight, it's a mishmash of 1970s glam gear, from Womble feet to Bay City Rollers trousers. All the Top 10 chart positions are held by Goodies records, and the Queen awards them all OBEs.

Made Pop Group Laureate, nationalised and ordered to cheer up the nation, they run foul of the Myth Inspectors and a nationwide ban on laughter, a ban that, hurtfully, ignores the real Tony Blackburn. The final outcome is a puppet government and 'Graeme and I just came up with the idea of a hand-puppet government'.

Before the Christmas broadcast, the BBC had fanned the flames by running an extensive repeat season of series five. The Goodies had also lived up to their names when, thanks to Tim, they were involved in the Derby Festival and took part in a tea party with Paddington Bear at Paddington Station in aid of Action Research for the Crippled Child.

In 'Goodies Rule – O.K' they were given access to every children's character at the corporation. 'We had

The Bootles. The missing link in the history of Mersey Beat!

Sooty as Prime Minister, Bill and Ben ganging up on Tim. Chequers was being run by characters from *Hector's House*. It worked really well,' says Bill. 'And if you just switch off from the visual stuff during the Dougal attack at the end and just listen to the soundtrack, it's amazing. During that whole puppet attack, if you just listen, there's some wonderful musicians working their rocks off on the music. The guitar is awesome!'

For Tim the scene proved rather gruesome. 'Now, after all these years, the truth can be told!' chuckles Bill. 'When that giant Zebedee landed between Tim's legs it didn't miss! He's not been a happy boy ever since!'

The episode ends with the real figures of British political power, Harold Wilson, Margaret Thatcher and Jeremy Thorpe, being controlled as puppets by the Goodies. The final image, however, is the Goodies as puppets being controlled by the ultimate puppet-master, Jim Franklin. 'There were times,' says Tim, 'when Jim would have loved it if we were puppets. He could have made us do anything and we wouldn't have complained or got hurt!'

'But for me,' says Bill, 'looking back on the episode it appears like a dream. For the three of us the best thing about *The Goodies* was dreaming up things and making those dreams come true. And what better dream could one have than kicking a Womble in the nuts!'

D We'll Show You Definitely.

CHARITY AND DAYLIGHT ROBBERY

Hot on the heels of the biggest year in *The Goodies*' history, the programme was making inroads into America. Broadcast on the Eastern Educational Network, according to Graeme, 'I believe we've got quite a good review … [but] it has taken the Americans rather a long time to make up their minds about us.'

Not so James Gilbert (Head of Comedy, Light Entertainment, Television) who commissioned seven more scripts in January 1976. Although it had been mooted that the 'Goodies Series V', as it was internally referred to, was only to comprise six episodes, Jim Franklin confirmed with contracts

Y You Should Employ Us Please

Bring back Engelbert! Tim's retro rant in the ultra-rare 'Hype Pressure' doesn't impress his colleagues.

manager John Moore 'that another series of seven *Goodies* episodes will be filmed from 29 March–30 April. Followed by rehearsals and studio recordings commencing 31 May–17 July. In addition to this the artists will be required for at least two days' preplanning during February/March and also for film dubbing during May.'

Jim Franklin mapped out three consecutive planning meetings from 25 February at Sangers in Lime Grove. He had 'been informed by Visual Effects, Design and Wardrobe Depts that if we are any later … [we] will not be ready to start shooting on 29 March. If you [the Goodies] consider these dates to be impossible, I will put the filming back sufficiently to accommodate. This should not put you out at the other end because we should not be shooting beyond 7 May.' Clearly, the team had a lot of clout.

'It was,' Bill believes, 'very important that we were so involved. We would even help with the editing. Well, I say help. I would usually say, "If you do it like it says in the script, it will work!" The really good editors didn't mind. But I'm sure we got quite annoying sometimes. But it was thanks to the BBC. Because we were so involved with every aspect of the show, we knew about the sound and the lighting. As a result, during studio recordings, we would get cross during breaks. We would say to the audience, "Do you wanna know why we have to do it again?" We were probably quite awkward and I'm sure some people were muttering about the artistes getting involved in it. But it was our show!'

It was money that would prove the stumbling block. On 28 January, James Gilbert, John Moore and Jim Franklin shared the following correspondence:

Goodies maestro Jim Franklin discusses the script with his star cast.

As expected we are having difficulty over fees for the next series, we haven't even got to the offer stage for I have learned from the agent of Oddie and Garden that they insist on parity with Tim Brooke-Taylor. Tim Brooke-Taylor has built up his fee with such series as 'Marty Feldman', 'Broaden Your Mind', 'Cliff Richard [The Case]', 'Rough and the Smooth' etc., to £400 on the last series while Garden was £300 and Oddie £270. Since that series, Tim has done 'Hallo [sic] Cheeky',

Variety appearances, and even playing the lead in a 'Shades of Green' [The Overnight Bag], while the other two have not done anything. This would entitle Tim to a slight increase, if we offered £25, which is less than 10%, giving the other two parity, they would have an increase of £125 and £155

respectively or 41% and 58%. This is assuming Tim accepts only a £25. You will recall that after a long struggle they had parity on the Christmas Special. Will you please advise me on what I should offer. Incidentally, Tim Brooke-Taylor's agent does not feel that he should have parity.

Still, the Goodies seemed reassuringly unchanged: when Jim Franklin's secretary Liz Cranston wrote to them in March 1976, she reflected in Graeme's letter that she was 'sorry to hear you've had the flu – hope you're feeling better'. For Tim it was, 'hope you had a lovely time skiing', and for Bill, 'hope you've enjoyed your bird-watching'.

Indeed, for the trio themselves, financial gain was the last thing on their minds when they were summoned for an important charity appearance…

A POKE IN THE EYE (WITH A SHARP STICK)

To mark the fifteenth anniversary of Amnesty International in 1976, the organisation had approached John Cleese the previous year with a view to staging a special fundraiser. With the star comedian having promised to rope in 'a couple of friends' the seed was sown for the granddaddy of all comedy charity spectaculars. Cheekily referred to as 'An Evening without David Frost', Cleese's 'couple of friends' turned out to be all of his fellow *Monty Python* team-mates (save Eric Idle), a reunion of *Beyond the Fringe* (with the exception of Dudley Moore), Eleanor Bron, Neil Innes, Barry Humphries and all of the Goodies. Still basking in pop stardom, they were called upon to perform four numbers, 'Mummy I Don't Like My Meat', 'Cactus in My Y-Fronts', 'Sick Man Blues' and 'The Funky Gibbon'. Under the direction of Jonathan Miller, the production took over Her Majesty's Theatre in London's West End for three sell-out concerts.

Aptly enough, it opened on April Fool's Day 1976. The final performance, on Saturday, 3 April, saw a below-par Tim, having yelled himself hoarse during the afternoon's FA Cup semi-final, which had seen his beloved Derby County lose to Manchester United. Still, it was Bill's vocals that carried the team through. Bill also joined the *Monty Python* team in a resurrection of the *Cambridge Circus* favourite, 'Humour Without Tears', while all the Goodies were drafted into Michael Palin's backing group for the closing performance of 'The Lumberjack Song'.

Roger Graef's *Omnibus* film for the BBC was screened on 29 December 1976, enjoying a low-key theatrical release in America under the rather uninspired, but indisputably commercial, title of *Monty Python Meets Beyond the Fringe*.

Transatlantic Records released an album of concert highlights. The Goodies were restricted to just one performance, that of 'The Funky Gibbon', although Bill in particular maintained that the recording was of poor quality and fought for the inclusion of 'Sick Man Blues' instead. The sheer popularity of 'The Funky Gibbon' won out and remained the sole Goodies contribution to

ROGER GRAEF'S
PLEASURE AT HER MAJESTY'S with

the Martin Lewis produced disc, although in 1991 Castle Communications released a double album featuring all four Goodies songs.

The gurus of post war British comedy, including Neil Innes and Bill, rallied round for Amnesty International.

eese • Peter Cook • Jonathan Miller • Alan Bennett
dies • Eleanor Bron • Barry Humphries ᴬⁿESSENTIAL Release

SEASIDE SPECIAL

The Goodies journeyed to Blackpool to record an appearance for the first of a new series on 13 June 1976. Staged in the Big Top of Gerry Cottle's Circus, it was billed as 'The Ken Dodd Blackpool Centenary Show'. Produced by Michael Hurll, the show also featured the *Are You Being Served?* team, Charlie Cairoli and Tony Blackburn and was broadcast on BBC1 on 19 June.

'Every schoolboy has some sort of dream – playing football for England, discovering a new wonder drug, marrying a film star – but, above all, being a member of a pop group,' explains Tim. 'And thanks to Bill's songs that's what we did, even to the extent, and this was every schoolboy's dream, of appearing on *Top of the Pops* and making friends with Pan's People. On one wonderful occasion we appeared on *Seaside Special* in Blackpool and [were filmed] going on the rides at the funfair with the Young Generation. On the outside we were sad old men, but on the inside we were the business.'

THE BAFTAS

The Goodies* was nominated as the Best Light Entertainment Programme and, although the show lost out to *Fawlty Towers*, the BBC had agreed terms with Thames Television to broadcast a clip during the coverage on 17 March 1976.

Series 6, Episode 1

LIPS, OR, ALMIGHTY COD

First broadcast: Tuesday, 21 September 1976, 9 p.m.

The Eskimos (Al Fiorgal, Mike Lee Lane, Stan Van, Rex Wei and Tony Calvert) extend their fishing limits by 2,000 miles and have a cod war with the Goodies in the Serpentine: and then Graeme breeds an enormous cod...

The big box-office hit of 1975 had been *Jaws* and Bill was keen to write a spoof. Graeme was less keen, believing any parody the team could offer now was out-dated. 'I was wrong,' admits Graeme. 'I thought we had missed the boat from the previous year. But *Jaws* has remained part of the culture. We could do a take on it now and still be relevant.' The joke was heightened by the use of the infamous *Jaws* theme. The Geoff Love

Orchestra recording from Big Terror Movie Themes was used!

'As well as the cultural thing,' reflects Bill, 'we also had the topical thing of the cod wars. We named the giant cod Brian because Graeme and I had an agent at the time called Brian Cod. That's an in-joke, that is!'

The reaction of 251 viewers was reflected in the Audience Research report:

Although ... pleased to see the return of The Goodies, this was, for a number of those reporting, a disappointing start to the new series. Remembering some of the inspired lunacy from last year, one group found the programmes laboured and 'flat' by comparison, almost as if the writers

Bill follows the rules of Let's Talk Eskimo; credited to S. Kimo Nell.

Biting the hand that feeds it; Brian attacks fish-farmer Graeme.

were struggling for ideas; others commented that it was silly, childish or just plain daft, finding little to laugh at in such 'schoolboy' antics.

Nevertheless, if not, perhaps, at their funniest, the Goodies had amused and entertained most of the sample. This was just their kind of humour, viewers often remarked – zany, off-beat, utterly ridiculous, of course, but all the funnier for being so – and the Goodies' send-up of Jaws (involving a monster cod) was quite hilarious, they thought. The visual humour – the trio being pursued by the giant fish, for instance – was, as always, particularly good, it was said, and the programme as a whole was fast-moving, inventive and great fun.

There was little specific comment on their performance but the Goodies were their usual excellent selves, it seemed, and all aspects of the production were approved, especially the 'very clever' camera work.

To sum up, then, although by no means the best of The Goodies, the show had usually been quite enjoyed – and, as one said, 'They are so likeable one can forgive a few lapses.'

Series 6, Episode 2

HYPE PRESSURE

First broadcast: Tuesday, 28 September 1976, 9 p.m.

It's the 1950s revival, Goodies style, with Tim in the director's chair. Bill and Graeme are overwhelmed and undermined, until they too take a hand in directing.

Taking the trend for vintage rock'n'roll just that little bit further, the team resurrects *Six-Five Special,* teddy boys, Brylcreem and Muffin the Mule. Laudably, classic names from 1950s BBC broadcasting were also put into the mix. Broadcaster McDonald Hobley was paid £85 for his appearance and assured that a 'now appearing in *No Sex Please, We're British* at the Strand Theatre, London' announcement would play over the closing credits.

Vintage announcer Sylvia Peters was also requested, but her role eventually went to fellow BBC pioneer Mary Malcolm. Jim Franklin wrote to her: 'I am delighted to hear that you will be appearing in *The Goodies* in an

episode which sends up the fifties. As you will see from the script, you make a brief appearance and things go wrong. We have already had your friend McDonald Hobley in the filming, and his contribution was very amusing.' The costume and make-up sheet required 'Sylvia Peters or whoever' to be made up 'as she was'.

A performance of 'Bless This House' on *Stars On Sunday* by Moira Anderson (Pauline Mee) is interrupted when Tim's literal director cues a barrage of bricks. The costume requirement noted that she should be wearing 'an awful evening dress'. Tim finally reverts further back, to the 1940s, and re-enacts World War Two with Hitler and the entire British army at his disposal. Graeme and Bill counter-battle with Vanessa Redgrave (Dawn Rodriques) and Red Indian footage gleaned from *They Died With Their Boots On,* before Tim unleashes Kitten Kong. Bill cues the giant Dougal. But the battle can't withstand the ultimate deterrent: Margaret Thatcher's party political broadcast.

The Good Old Days. Tim goes 1940s mad with hilarious results, although Bill is clearly not amused. Graeme, meanwhile, shows signs of being a conscientious objector.

DAYLIGHT ROBBERY ON THE ORIENT EXPRESS

First broadcast: Tuesday, 5 October 1976, 9 p.m.

Listen to the band! The Goodies keep cheerful after the Orient Express lets them down.

Goodies 'Adventure Tours' give a detectives' club a world tour in a stationary railway coach. The illusion is almost complete ... but then they are hijacked.

Classic crime fever was at a peak following the 1974 film *Murder on the Orient Express*, which directly inspired Tim's performance as Ingrid Bergman! The Goodies round up every literal and televisual detective they can think of, with notable appearances from Ironside (Eric Kent), Sherlock Holmes (Trevor Wedlock), Kojak (John Repsch), Lord Peter Wimsey (Phillip Grant)

and at least seven Hercule Poirots, four of whom are played by Goodies regular Fred Tomlinson! Best of all is Miss Marple (Mary Andow), who benefits from Tim's vocals in the style of Lady Constance.

With a stuffed cow, a moveable tree and a mini Eiffel Tower, the Goodies keep their customers entertained, but nothing can save them when the train goes missing and the group find themselves in the Cannes Le Boring Festival. A rival troupe chill the blood with the threat of a six-and-a-half-hour mime version of *Murder on the Orient Express*, but, in a wry comment on the Montreux Festival, the Goodies benefit from the help of (Jimmy) Gilbert the goat!

Series 6, Episode 4

BLACK AND WHITE BEAUTY

First broadcast: Tuesday, 12 October 1976, 9 p.m.

The Goodies run their pantomime horse in the Grand National. Bill is jockey, Tim and Graeme provide motive power and the rest of the field have dubious pedigrees.

Graeme's half of the script delights in a Pet's Corner full of stuffed animals all called Kenneth, while Bill's contribution is a crossbreed between *Black Beauty* and *National Velvet*. With *All Creatures Great and Small* the latest cosy BBC hit for Sunday evenings, the Goodies fearlessly rip into the beloved vet show by revealing James Herriott's latest effort, 'How to Drown Kittens'.

'We had always been pretty cruel to animals,' says Bill, 'which is a bit ironic really. But the only complaint we ever got was because of my whipping of the pantomime horse. Some old dear wrote in saying, "How dare Bill Oddie mistreat that poor defenceless creature." We wrote back and said it was Tim and Graeme in a skin! "Oh, that's all right then!"'

Today Bill is one of BBC's most respected and prolific naturalists. Although happy to muck about for *Return of the Goodies* in 2005 he observed, 'they don't ask David Attenborough to do this, do they!' But he admits that, 'I was always into wildlife, but it's odd when your life-long hobby and passion becomes your job.'

'Tomorrow when one rides him for the first time I know it's going to be the thrill of one's lifetime.' 'Yes. My, my, listen to that wind.' 'Sorry, it's just that I'm so excited!'

Series 6, Episode 5

IT MIGHT AS WELL BE STRING

First broadcast: Tuesday, 19 October 1976, 9.10 p.m.

The Goodies run an advertising agency and find that honesty does not pay. So they advertise string and bring about commercial disaster.

The comic commercial is back with a vengeance with an entire episode devoted to them. The targets were as instantly recognisable as ever, with Graeme's 'Captain Fishface, based on Captain Birdseye, of course'.

Any boring old thing can be revived via a sexy ad campaign and suddenly string is the thing. *Tomorrow's World* host, Raymond Baxter, pops up in string underwear and presents a rock guitarist employing real string for his instrument, and demonstrates the rather inferior string umbrella. Bill sings 'I'd Like to Teach the World to String' and even Tim's Beans Boy makes a return appearance to advertise string.

Tim ultimately gets trapped in a world of interlocking commercials, perhaps most memorably giving into seduction in the Kung Poo aftershave ad. It employed original Hai Karate girl, Valerie Leon, who gives Tim a few karate chops for his trouble.

As if to emphasise the trio's understanding of television completely, the final scene has them crowded round their set. The point-of-view shot is from behind the screen as the credits roll and Jim Franklin's name appears. 'He's to blame,' says Bill.

'Trying to win a prize,' comments Tim knowingly.

'He won't!' mutters Graeme, as he switches off the set.

Series 6, Episode 6

2001 AND A BIT

First broadcast: Tuesday, 26 October 1976, 9 p.m.

Era 2001. The new generation of Goodies rediscover the ancient game of cricket and stage the match of the century – MCC (retired) versus Rollerball.

Reflecting on what life would be like when they are in their sixties, the team predict a world where violence is the thing. And, in a bizarre scene, they play versions of each other: Bill is Tim, Tim plays Graeme and Graeme is Bill. For Graeme it leaves memories of 'very prickly facial hair'.

The original Tim seems to be the father of all three of the new Goodies, while the mother was Racquel Welsh! But it's the old guard that stands up and gets counted. Chanting about the MCC and resurrecting the ancient art of cricket, the vintage Goodies are still seen as an unquenchable force, even strolling through the post-nuclear mushroom cloud.

Still, the most affectionate moment comes as the aged Goodies reminiscence: 'The three-seater bike, you remember the good old days ... ooh yes, the giant kitten. The giant beanstalk. The ministry of silly walks. I don't remember that!'

Graeme, in Bill mode, gets down and dirty in the 21st century.

THE GOODIES GREATEST

Bradley's Records capped the Goodies' chart career with a compilation of the six singles released between the end of 1974 and the beginning of 1976. Four of the B-sides were also included, alongside a slight variation on 'The Goodies Theme' and a previously unreleased Goodies version of Bill's 'Charles Aznovoice', a number previously heard in *I'm Sorry I'll Read That Again*.

GOODY LOCATIONS

The Torquay Cricket Club doubled for the MCC in '2001 and a Bit', while 'Black and White Beauty' used Newton Abbot racecourse.

Series 6, Episode 7

THE GOODIES ALMOST LIVE

First broadcast: Tuesday, 2 November 1976, 9 p.m.

Also referred to as 'Goodies in Concert', this episode proved a truncated bone of contention between the BBC and the Goodies themselves. When the series was commissioned, Jimmy Gilbert had requested that all seven scripts be delivered by 16 February 1976. In the event, Jim Franklin noted on 7 May 1976: 'That six out of the seven 'Goodies' scripts have been accepted. The usual payments may now be made.'

However, despite the concert show going into the studio on 17 July, Gilbert was not satisfied, subsequently, that it counted as the seventh episode of the series.

Agent Roger Hancock wrote on 19 August: 'I have now had further discussions with the writers, who assure me that our request for a half fee is more than fair. Apart from the inclusion of original written material, the programme has required very careful structuring and is not as you suggested to me the other day "a Variety Act"!'

Best of ... the Goodies **was released in Australia in 1976**

However, the Head of Copyright Antony Jennings was not convinced:

I am afraid I cannot agree. We commissioned the writers for seven 'specially written' television scripts and we did expect that they would write original material. If you have seen the seventh script you will realise that they did not provide original material but compiled a show based largely on previously written material, much of which had been included in their LP [The Goodies Greatest]. Consequently, we do not consider payment for 'specially written' script material to be justified. When we spoke on the telephone, I drew an analogy between entertainers who put together a Variety Show using their existing material and the seventh 'Goodies in Concert' script. This seems to me to be reasonable. In neither case should we be expected to pay scriptwriters for such 'structuring'.

Of course, you must speak for your clients, but as you will know the writers had previously agreed in discussing this with Jimmy Gilbert that they had not provided an original script in the way in which they had been commissioned and accepted that the half fee already paid should be offset against a future commission. I am sorry that there should be this disagreement about the material for this programme and it is naturally not intended to be any reflection on the writers. We do feel strongly, however, that you are asking for payment in circumstances where it is not warranted.

Indeed, the script slavishly reproduced Bill's lyrics for such classic numbers as 'The Inbetweenies', 'Black Pudding Bertha' and 'Nappy Love'. The 'structuring' amounted to little more than a Pan's Grannies preamble and a brief run through dance crazes like the Funky Chicken and the Loony Moth as a build-up to a performance of 'The Funky Gibbon'.

On 7 September Hancock insisted, 'I understand that no discussion took place with Jimmy Gilbert regarding the fee for this episode and certainly our clients do not accept that the half fee already paid should be offset against a future commission.' A week later Jennings was adamant. 'Perhaps you would remind your clients of the conversation they had with Jimmy Gilbert at 4 p.m. on Wednesday, 23 June and the understanding that was reached.'

Hancock didn't respond until 20 October, when he assured Jennings, 'I have spoken yet again to our clients who have no recollection of the conversation with Jimmy Gilbert.' The following week Jennings wrote:

I am sorry this correspondence is becoming so protracted and is rather moving away from the central point, which is that we do not feel that the script for the seventh programme in the series was such as would justify a fee under the terms of the Agreement for an original series and serials episode. However, I must deal with your letter of 20 October, which is frankly astonishing. I have today talked with Jimmy Gilbert's office and the meeting was indeed noted in his diary and was attended by Tim Brooke-Taylor, Graeme Garden and Bill Oddie. Indeed, I remember clearly that Jimmy spoke to me about the meeting shortly afterwards, isn't it odd?

There the correspondence ends. And the show, referred to internally as 'The "LP" script' was duly included as the seventh episode of the sixth series.

NOTHING TO DO WITH US!

'We defected to Island Records,' remembers Bill. 'That was my fault. And it was a fault because it kind of killed us off as pop stars. I know for a fact that Tim and Graeme weren't too happy with me about that. But it was my terrible muso side coming out and I thought we were becoming terribly soppy under Bradley's Records. I wanted us to be taken a little bit more seriously. I was going to start recording straight songs under the Goodies banner. I had serious things to say about serious subjects … and 'Blowing Off!' To be perfectly honest Island Records was a very hip record company. I mean, they had Bob Marley and the Wailers and all those sort of people on their books. That was reason enough to go with them. Just to say I had been with Island Records was enough to sacrifice everything. And that's pretty much what I did. It was, musically, the best record we ever made … by a mile!'

In November, 'Blowing Off' and 'Elisabeth Rules – U.K!' formed the only single from the album. Although it failed to chart, 'I really didn't care,' says Bill. 'I suppose if I'm going to get all pretentious on you, this was the Goodies concept album. We had some very good musicians on it. It was a dream to work with musicians that I liked and that I admired and that I knew. We had people from Joe Cocker's band. Rick Wakeman did a couple of tracks. Some really big names played on it, which was lovely. I purposely wrote all the songs for the album. It wasn't a case of digging out things we had used for incidental music on the show. This was an album that I planned. It was called *Nothing To Do With Us!* because it was fairly scurrilous and there were sexy songs ["She Wouldn't Understand"] and drug songs ["I Wish I Could Get High"] and farting songs ["Blowing Off", with farting provided by bass player Billy Kristian] and all sorts of things like that on it. "The Policeman's Opera" was this attack on police brutality. Actually, that's my favourite Goodies record of all time. It was a complete pipe dream of myself and Dave MacRae, who was my musical director on the show and who produced the album. Tim and Graeme hardly turned up at all, to be honest. They didn't really need to be

there because they just did their little bit of vocals and some silly voices and then I told them to bugger off! I used to love the hours in the studio and, sad sod that I am, fairly recently I found a cassette of it and played it in the car and it stands up surprisingly well. It was a send up of "Bohemian Rhapsody"

and that kind of thing. The big Queen-type epic production. It's massive … absolutely massive. There's a great guitar solo by Bernie Holland. The track goes on for about twelve minutes and I absolutely love it!'

'But,' admits Bill, 'that was it for us as rock stars, I'm afraid. I suppose the problem was at Island Records. We could never actually find anybody. There was this marijuana haze down at their place and we could never find anybody to promote the record. In fact, after a couple of weeks of working there, I remember coining the phrase that the staff of Island Records seemed rather more keen on turning on than turning up!'

BOUNCE

As if to prove how successful 1975 had been for the Goodies, the start of 1976 revealed that the team had been the sixth biggest-selling rock group in the country for the year. Bill Oddie, consequently, was the fifth most successful songwriter. Amazing then to consider that the glory days were already over. This was the last Goodies single released by Bradley's Records in a continuation of The New Goodies LP promotion, although only the B-side – 'Good Ole Country Music' – was featured on the release. The A-side was a re-recorded version of the song featured in 'Goodies Rule – O.K'

DISNEY TIME

The Goodies were contracted on 12 December 1976 'to link film excerpts and provide own material' for the Boxing Day special for producer/director Richard Evans, broadcast from 5.50 p.m. on BBC1. Filmed at the department store, Selfridges, the trio presented clips from such classics as *Bambi*, *Cinderella* and *Dumbo*, and new releases *The Shaggy D.A.*, *Treasure of Matecumbe* and *Ride a Wild Pony*.

The Goodies plead innocence over their most 'scurrilous' recording; and hang out with the world's most famous mouse.

Goodies. Goody Goody Yum Yum.

THE BIG BANG

At the start of the year, the Goodies were in a buoyant mood. Their music career seemed to have matured with a signing to Island Records. From March, the BBC was dutifully running an extensive repeat season, including the whole of the sixth series and specially selected classics from the fifth. And, to top it all, the newspapers were ripe with inspiration. From the Queen's Silver Jubilee to the gob-inducing invasion of punk rock, the Goodies had plenty of targets for their comic barbs.

As Bill had observed: 'What we are doing is projecting our own humour. We write it and we act it, so we are projecting ourselves. Consequently, it is much nicer than if someone comes up and says, "Excuse me, aren't you Ena Sharples?"'

'Yes, I can see you would find that a bit irritating,' noted Graeme.

Goodies. We're coming for you.

The writing process was unchanged. 'We may start off with a list of about twenty ideas for one show,' revealed Graeme, 'but by the end of the meeting only two or three will end up going in. That's because the rest are so rotten. From there we will spend about two days working out the plot and the joke sequences, then we'll go to the visual effects department and the props department to see if we can make the ideas work. Sometimes it's a toss-up whether the ideas go to costumes or props.'

For Tim, being a Goody could make one think. 'We were doing this sketch which involved me pretending to be a dog and, as I was crawling about on all fours with a stick in my mouth, it suddenly occurred to me that I did have a degree! The trouble is people expect a professional man to be serious. They would be very upset by a lawyer who came in wearing a revolving bow tie and a carnation that squirted water in your eye.'

On 29 March 1977, Jimmy Gilbert wrote: 'I should be grateful if you would go ahead and commission six 'Goodies' scripts (at thirty minutes each).' Both the BBC and the Goodies themselves still continued to perceive the split third and fourth series as one batch of episodes rather than two. Thus, on scripts and in correspondence, these new programmes were discussed as the sixth series rather than the seventh. It was contractually agreed to start filming on 5 September, although the schedule was delayed until the Friday of that week, with location work completed by 14 October.

With Jim Franklin regaining a tight hold on the production, the film direction was assigned to Bob Spiers.

MICHAEL BARRATT

(1928–)

A respected broadcaster who first came to prominence on television as a reporter on *Panorama*, Barratt was a key interviewer for the coverage of the 1964 General Election. However, it was as the anchorman for *Nationwide* from 1969 until 1977 that he remains best remembered. More than happy to appear on *The Goodies*, Tim recalls, 'His interview with the Prime Minister Sooty [in 'Goodies Rule – O.K'] was one of my favourite moments. Michael played it perfectly. Deadpan and for real. He knew the joke would be enough to make his performance funny.' He also played himself in 'Kung Fu Kapers', 'Scoutrageous' and 'Punky Business'.

THE MAKING OF THE GOODIES' DISASTER MOVIE

As if to dismiss the 1974 *Goodies Annual* completely, this was dubbed the 'Goodies book III' by the group. Published by Weidenfeld and Nicolson, it rips the lid off the British Film Industry via the preproduction hell of the Goodies' break into movies. It showcases the proposed romp *Carry On Christ*, reveals the censored funny three seconds of *Confessions of a Window Cleaner* and pleads for a break from Walt Disney, with Tim giving his love to Thumper. Adding a flourish of Alfred Hitchcock showmanship, it is planned to tag the film with 'The Goodies Are Coming', although they admit that sexy starlets help with finance; Sheikh Yafist puts up a lot for Rita Acapulco's appearance! Originally scheduled for an autumn 1976 publication to

be followed by their feature film debut, the failure of the film within the book was a sad reflection of the failure of the proposed *Goodies* film by master filmmaker Steven Spielberg. It was to relate how the Goodies met.

'We got a call from Spielberg's office asking whether we would be interested in doing a film!' says Tim. 'Once we had recovered from the shock and made sure it wasn't a joke, we said, "Yes, of course." Time went on and on and, sadly, he made a comedy which didn't do very well [*1941* (1979)] and he went cold on the idea.'

'I think he thought aliens and dinosaurs were more likely box-office winners,' muses Bill.

Series 7, Episode 1

ALTERNATIVE ROOTS

First broadcast: Tuesday, 1 November 1977, 9 p.m.

The Goodies delve into their ancestry, and discover entwined roots and crossed paths leading inexorably back to a strange circular edifice.

'*The Black and White Minstrel Show* was the most popular programme on telly at the time,' says Bill. 'No one can believe that now, but it was huge... We just mixed it with *Roots*, threw in a load of multicoloured minstrels and there you are.'

The Northern roots of the trio are reflected with Graeme's Scottish background exposed in the hunt for the haggis in 'Hoots', Bill's cider-drinking tribe examined in 'Froots', and Tim's posh descendant of sheep-stealers joining the others in a slave market headed for such BBC horrors as *Seaside Special* and *The Max Bygraves Show*. Typically, the obsession affects the entire network, with 'Cocojak', 'Black Peter' and Michael Darkinson interviewing a white Mohammad Ali!

'As a result our show has been branded racist,' says Tim, 'but we were trying to highlight the absurdity of the Minstrels. The absurd thing was that we were tarred with the same brush.' The Goodies had an opportunity to discuss the new series and their new book on the evening this first episode was broadcast when they were interviewed on *Nationwide*.

Lordy, Lordy! A satirical swipe at a BBC family favourite.

Why can't it be *The White and White Minstrel Show*?'

'That would be racial prejudice.'

Series 7, Episode 2

DODONUTS

First broadcast: Tuesday, 8 November 1977, 9 p.m.

In which Bill tries to protect the last of the dodos, teaches it to fly, finds it a mate, and discovers the real reason for its extinction.

Tim and Graeme are the Colonel Blimp types with a blood lust to kill anything that walks or flies. Joined by bumbling fellow hunters (Barney Carroll, Rocky Newby, Ernie Goodyer and Eddie Davies) and relishing the Endangered Species Club overseen by Club Butler (Bill Gosling), it is down to Bill, as the eco-freak bird-watcher, to protect threatened creatures. The ultimate goal is, of course, the dodo. Bird-impersonator extraordinaire Percy Edwards was the obvious choice to provide the bird's vocals. Liz Cranston wrote to him: 'I enclose a copy of the second script in the forthcoming new series of *The Goodies*, which we would like you to look at with a view to doing some 'DODO' screeches for us!' Edwards was required for film dubbing on 26 October, rehearsals five days later, and studio recording on 4 November.

Both Tim and Bill don dodo disguises, with the costume and make-up plot noting that Tim's 'dodo disguise looks pretty awful – long johns, tufts of feathers, huge flipper feet'. It was agreed that visual effects 'will do rubber beak'. They were also to 'do Mickey Mouse ears, which are fixed to his hat' for Tim's 'Disney Cameraman Silent Movie type' for the parody of the popular *True Life Adventures*.

But, according to the Audience Research Department report on the episode, it was undoubtedly the squawking, crapping, peeing dodo that delighted viewers. 'Many praised the special effects and the "dodo" was a particular favourite, amusing very many. Just one or two felt that the speeded-up items went on a bit too long, while an equally small number thought some of the sketches were just too silly. Nevertheless, for most, this week's programme had made enjoyable viewing.'

Series 7, Episode 3

SCOUTRAGEOUS

First broadcast: Tuesday, 22 November 1977, 9 p.m.

The Goodies go scouting and gain their proficiency badges. But their initiatives cost more than a bob-a-job and cause Tim a change of uniform.

The darker side of the Boy Scout movement is 'exposed', with Witch-Finder General-inspired Scout-Finder General (Frank Windsor). Bill's desire to get the 'Cheering Up Lonely Housewives Whose Husbands Are At Work' badge, and aged scouts (Norman Bacon, Barney Carroll, Eddie Davies, Ernie Goodyer and James Muir) giving themselves a cold shower at the merest naughty thought. Moreover, it was feared that Tim's leadership of the Salvation Army would cause offence but, he believed, 'The only people who will be offended by jokes about the Salvation Army are, bizarrely, those non-religious members of the audience.'

Max Bygraves avoided further *Goodies* attack when a joke about sticking Graeme's home-made atom bomb under him was altered to affect Oliver Reed instead. The rehearsal script also featured Bill making rude words in semaphore and Graeme tying knots in Tim's lanyard as part of his overzealous bob-a-job week. Jo Kendall, a familiar voice from *I'm Sorry I'll Read That Again*, is heard once more as the voice of Corporal Cleanly, while Bill's costume has a familiar ring about it as well. His oversized hat was recycled from 'Scatty Safari' and his sparkling jacket was previously worn by John Inman in *Are You Being Served?* ('The Old Order Changes').

PUNKY BUSINESS

First broadcast: Tuesday, 29 November 1977, 9 p.m.

The Goodies go punk. At the Trendsetters Ball, Tim puts his best foot forward and gains the hand of a lady.

Suitably for an episode that tackles two very different strands of popular music, the show is known under two further titles. 'Rock Goodies' was clearly inspired by the popular Thames drama, *Rock Follies*. Indeed, the costume sheet notes: 'Bill is in a purple singlet and patched jeans ... Graeme casual, but with a bubble wig. Tim in a silk dressing gown but with a spiky black

Jane Asher joining in the fun.

wig ... not unlike Julie Covington.' Covington starred as Dee in *Rock Follies* and, because of disputes over regional broadcasts, 'Punky Business' was shown directly opposite it.

Tim, Graeme and Bill joined forces with Dave MacRae to record the vocals for the songs 'Rock Goodies', 'On the Road' and the brief sting 'Goodies Split'. The script requested that the screen writing should be 'in Rock Follies style blue neon letters'. It was further noted: 'The first half of the show should look and sound and feel like *Rock Follies*... This first scene should probably be pretaped and edited so it can have jump cuts and rather mannered overlay etc.'

Still, the musical highlight is Bill's performance of the Paddy Roberts and Jack Goodman ballad 'I'm In Love for the Very First Time'. Credited to George and Ira Gershwin in the stage directions, Bill was obviously not convinced, adding, 'Check who wrote it! And also can we find the sheet music please so I can work out the routine.' The dance material was choreographed by Flick Colby, who was best known for her Pan's People routines.

Moreover, the Goodies were planning a stage show designed to promote the team as a pop group, although Tim and Graeme wanted to include sketch material as well. 'I had sat in as substitute drummer for bands in the early days of *The Goodies*,' says Bill, 'but the natural move was for us to go on the road. We never did, but I did do solo gigs at the time. Tim and Graeme came and saw my show at the Rainbow Club in Highbury. That was wonderful: Jimi Hendrix, Queen, Stevie Wonder, the Jackson Five and me have played that venue! It was actually not the right place for my kind of stuff. What was far more appropriate was over a dozen campus gigs, which were great fun. I played Glasgow on a Saturday

Even Tim's shiny shoes can't stop the musical decline of the Goodies.

night and lived! Looking back, I fell under the spell of doing the rock act for real. I was doing all the silly songs but dressing in that glam rock fashion. I was a lot slimmer in those days and was dangerously bordering on a rock image. I should have just done a Billy Connolly in T-shirt and jeans, but it was the glam era. I got T-shirts made by the same people who worked on *Rock Follies*. They were based in Cricklewood as it happens. I had "Wild Thing" and the like emblazoned across them. My daughter, Rosie, sometimes borrows them to this day!'

The second alternative title, 'Punkarella', reflects punk rock in pantomime terms. Caroline Kook (Jane Asher) was inspired by Caroline Coon, the celebrated *Melody Maker* journalist who was stepping out with The Clash's Paul Simonon at the time. Bill Grumpy (Roland MacLeod) parodies *Today* host Bill Grundy, who suffered a memorable encounter with the Sex Pistols. And Graeme enjoys his manic practice at St Punk's Hospital with his punk nurse (*'Allo, 'Allo*'s Vicki Michelle) who, in

an unused scene, is actually revealed to have once been Michael Parkinson!

'We were called in to the BBC and told we couldn't make the show!' says Graeme. 'Bill and I knew we were sailing fairly close to the wind. We even wrote in a couple of lines we knew would get cut just to see if we could get away with it. [In a scene in the back of a police van, glue sniffing was referenced – 'a cheeky little glue!' – while another hospital scene saw a patient (Mike Mungarven) who has had his hands set in concrete.] But we didn't expect total censorship. The idea was that, by 1977, punk rock had pushed beyond all known boundaries. We were pushing it that little bit further. That was funny to us. The BBC couldn't understand that the whole point of the show was to take punk and push it to its most disgusting and revolting conclusion.'

Finally it was Tim that successfully argued the point with Jimmy Gilbert, with Bill as mediator.

Series 7, Episode 5

ROYAL COMMAND

First broadcast: Tuesday, 6 December 1977, 9 p.m.

The Goodies, by Royal Command, stage a variety show, invade the Palace, create a coronation, cause diversions in the Mall and lose a three-seater bike.

Originally scheduled to go out on 15 November, in a series riddled with controversy, this mockery of the royal family in the Queen's Jubilee year was one step too far for the BBC. 'We had the Royals sleeping through a Royal Command Performance – which I'm sure they did,' says Graeme. 'We had footage of the Royals falling off horses – The Amazing Tumbling Royals [with riding stunts by 'Bronco' McLaughlin and Max Faulkner]. Finally we stand in for the Royals because they are all bandaged up in hospital. Tim even becomes the Queen. The problem was that two Royals were actually in hospital at the time. Alasdair Milne explained that Princess Anne was in hospital expecting a baby and said, "If she has her baby before six o'clock on the day the show is transmitted, then that show cannot go out!" I was tempted to say, "That begs the question, what do we do if she has her baby between six and the time the show goes out at nine?" Begging the answer, I supposed, that Alasdair Milne had gone home by that stage and thus it was not his responsibility!'

In the event the baby was born at 11.30 a.m. and a memo was issued saying: 'Due to the Royal flavour of episode three, which was to have been transmitted tonight, it has been decided to replace it with one of the last series.' The chosen episode was '2001 and a Bit' but, as Graeme says, the BBC didn't have a clue. 'Our administrator said, "I've got the solution, instead of putting this one out why don't you put out the one you recorded last Friday?" We said, "This *is* the one we recorded last Friday!"'

When the show finally went out, three weeks after it was originally scheduled, 296 viewers responded to the Audience Research questionnaire. Its findings revealed that '… only a small proportion (13%) of the sample did not find this episode funny and many of these objected to The Goodies using the Royal Family as a target for their comedy. This was felt to be in bad taste and unfair as the Royal Family could not hit back.' However, it went on: 'About 70% of those reporting considered this current series had been a success and some applauded the way certain Establishment sacred cows (both institutions and attitudes) became butts.'

A more worrying aspect of the feedback, though, was the 'definite, though not overwhelming, feeling that other series had been better. Some felt too much reliance was being placed on slapstick and sight gags to cover up the shortcomings in the storylines and scripts… Most of the sample were fairly enthusiastic about a further series and about three in ten were fairly opposed to a return.'

It wasn't quite the end, but with the Royals taking over the BBC, there is something poignant about Tim watching the four-seater trandem in the new series, 'The Royals'.

Tim's crowning moment as he becomes the Head of the Commonwealth.

Series 7, Episode 6

EARTHANASIA

First broadcast: Tuesday, 22 December 1977, 9 p.m.

A finale to the series. The Goodies on Christmas Eve – and the world is due to end at midnight … is this really their last thirty minutes?

What would turn out to be the bleakest Christmas comedy special ever begins with a seasonal tradition: Graeme decorating the tree. But a BBC newsflash soon shatters the illusion as world leaders have faced the inevitable and decided to eliminate the earth at midnight! As Bill says, 'If you can't think of a punch line – blow up the world!'

All performed in real time, the episode deconstructs the usual festive fare – too much telly, booze and grub – while allowing the trio to reflect on the ultimate question of 'What's it all about?'

For Bill, it was all about losing his hair. 'I had my usual beard and moustache for the recording, but we wrote in a scene where I shave it off. The world was about to end. It wasn't that big a deal in the great scheme of things. Anyway, the inevitable thing happened. We were halfway through the recording, I had half a beard on and someone rushed in shouting, "Hold it!" Jim Franklin had noticed a microphone boom in shot and wanted to re-record an earlier scene. I said, "Tough! So there's a boom in shot!" I ended the show completely bald. The joke was that the audience didn't laugh. I had done it for nothing!'

'A couple of minutes ago what was

I into? Violence, destruction, skate-boarding

through Christmas Trees!'

However, at least one viewer thought the whole thing was rather familiar. The repeat of the episode in the early spring of 1978 prompted David Marshall to write: 'The last programme of *The Goodies* screened about a fortnight ago was based on the idea of the world ending on Christmas Eve. A radio play of mine – *P.M. in the Morning* – based on the idea of the world ending on Christmas Eve, was broadcast in December 1976. Any comments?' It was noted that Jim Franklin would speak to one of the writers and an internal memo recorded: 'Oddie, through Franklin, said that he had never heard of either the author or the play.' This was slightly sweetened when a letter was despatched to Marshall: 'I understand that the producer of *The Goodies* has spoken to Bill Oddie, one of the writers of the sketch in question, and that Mr Oddie was not aware of your play. Any similarity between the two works is coincidence.'

Besides, it's unlikely that Marshall's play had the sheer joy of Graeme's mini re-enactment of *The Muppet Show* by using Tim's dirty washing or the emotive and touching conclusion as the allotted time comes and goes and it's revealed that Graeme has put the clock back thirty seconds so his pals can think the whole thing was a joke and die with a smile on their faces. The blast of white, the BBC globe symbolically exploding and the end credits rolling *sans* music is probably as powerful as British comedy has ever got.

'*The Goodies* hadn't exactly become a strain on us, but don't forget we were involved at every single level of the show,' says Bill. 'It was a blessed relief sometimes to have a nice, studio-bound show like the earth one, because during filming you had to be "on duty" all the time. I mean, at least one of us had to have his wits about him even if we weren't in the scene. It wasn't a case of not trusting our director or anything, it's just we knew exactly how *The Goodies* did and didn't work.'

Graeme reveals, 'We were secretly hoping that the end of *The Goodies* would get the same public response as the "death" of Sherlock Holmes. We thought that the public might jam the BBC switchboard screaming, "Don't finish *The Goodies* – they must come back … one day!" But nobody really noticed or, at least, took our destruction very seriously. I suppose we took delight from the fact that nobody actually phoned up and said, "Thank God that's over!"'

GOODIES FUN BOOK

As part of a 1977 promotional campaign by Cadbury's chocolates, kids with a sweet tooth could collect 100 Cadbury's wrappers and exchange them for a *Goodies* comic book from IPC Magazines. Featuring jokes, cartoons, Bill's nature page and Graeme's Garden Tips, two versions were produced: a junior one and another one for older children.

Here we come into town.

THE INBETWEENIES

1978-80

The final destruction of the Goodies and, indeed, the entire earth at Christmas 1977 was taken by the team as a signal to have a break. As Bill admits, 'A break was a very appealing thing. We didn't even have any plans for another series, although we never said, "That's it, then." Mind you, we had done a hell of a lot. We had to live a bit in order to write about life with some sort of life experience, if you understand me! And I suppose it was healthy for me to do something without the other two.'

Bill became the host of a new, wacky ITV children's programme, *The Saturday Banana*. 'The main reason for me doing it was to simply do something different from *The Goodies*. That show. That team. That had been my life for nearly ten years. And I also wanted to do *The Saturday*

Getting up, falling down.

Banana because a lot of children's programming at that time was so condescending. They were so safe. I wanted to do something a little different. And serious. Mind you, I had that whole thing of "How dare you try and be a children's presenter and not be funny. You're a comedian!"

Anyway, apparently kids found me funny even when I was trying to be serious, so I failed on that score as well!'

While Bill was keen to branch out alone, Tim and Graeme joined forces for a theatrical tour and West End run of *The Unvarnished Truth*. 'That was a joy,' reflects Graeme. 'It was complete madness, but a joy. It was just lovely to have a break from the total control and responsibility of *The Goodies*. Just to turn up and say other people's lines for a change.'

'I don't remember a planned break,' says Tim, 'but this was the beginning of the BBC not rushing to put us in the schedules. Jonathan Lynn, a former Footlights colleague and head of the Cambridge Theatre Company, invited Graeme and me to appear in a play called *The Unvarnished Truth*. The play was written by Royce Ryton, who had recently had huge success with *Crown Matrimonial*.

'My character was based on Royce himself and I was able to study the original as Royce and his wife Morah were also in the cast. It was enormous fun to do, but incredibly tiring for all concerned – nearly all the members of the cast had buckets of water poured over them.'

Tim was also involved in another comic team. 'When away from *The Goodies*, I was working mostly with John Junkin, a neighbour in London, and Barry Cryer. The three of us would spend very jolly days in John Junkin's flat writing *Hello Cheeky*. Living downstairs was our musical maestro, Denis King. It was a comedy squat – except for the fact that huge rents were paid. *Hello Cheeky* was a big success on radio, but died a death on

Bill got on his bike to host *The Saturday Banana*.

television. We tried too hard to make it visually slick on television when we should have shown the chaos that was really going on as we struggled into costumes and leaped into close-ups.'

Still, contrary to Tim's opinion at the time, the BBC was keen to get them back into a television studio. On 31 August 1978, agent Roger Hancock was informed: 'John Howard Davies ... would like to commission the lads to write seven more scripts for *The Goodies* to be delivered by the end of January 1979.' An offer of £3,000 per script, to cover two broadcasts, was deemed unacceptable, with thc team requesting a payment of £2,000 and a renegotiation rate with regards lucrative repeats.

Graeme and Bill had also received a special commission from John Howard Davies in September 1978. Produced and directed by Jim Franklin, *The Twenty-First Century Show* was to take a candid sideways glance at life in the year 2001. 'We weren't in it at all. It was an overt entry for Montreux,' explains Bill. Indeed, in BBC correspondence it is referred to as 'the Bill Oddie/Graeme Garden – Montreux Entry'.

'In theory you weren't supposed to make special programmes for the contest,' continues Bill. 'It had to be something which had already been broadcast, but Lew Grade and ATV finally cheated and won by editing down ten one-hour shows of Marty Feldman to a single twenty-one-minute programme. So the BBC commissioned Graeme and I to write this futuristic variety show. It was consciously written in a too-clever-by-half style purely to please lots of foreigners with no sense of humour! We had this elaborate weightless circus on the moon with elephants dressed in spacesuits floating off as they did their begging trick. It was very weird stuff, all done with models. One of my favourite bits was a sex scene done with test tubes, a touch of Woody Allen's *Sleeper*, I suppose. The scene was shot like a blue movie with Andrew Ray pouring liquid into different containers.'

Favourite *Goodies* baddie Henry McGee, along with Ann Hamilton and Judy Loe were in support, but although scheduled for a 12 April 1979 broadcast, the show was pulled at the eleventh hour. And, despite a BBC memo of September 1978 noting there was 'an agreement in principle', the new series of *The Goodies* was neglected in favour of the team's latest album.

ROLAND MACLEOD
(1935–)

As a writer and actor on *It's Marty* and *Broaden Your Mind*, MacLeod became very much part of the pre-*Goodies* world of Tim. Between 1970 ('Give Police a Chance') and 1980 ('A Kick in the Arts') he made seven appearances on *The Goodies*. The roles in-between were Peter Vest in 'Come Dancing', scientist James Burke in 'Invasion of the Moon Creatures', Sir Joshua Makepiece in 'Cunning Stunts', Swingometer host Robert McKenzie in 'Goodies Rule – O.K' and Bill Grumpy in 'Punky Business'. As a jobbing comedy actor, he appeared in Graham Chapman and Bernard McKenna's *Comedy Playhouse* ('Idle at Work'), *Sykes* ('Sykes and the Pub'), *Ripping Yarns* ('Escape from Stalag Luft 112B'), *Please, Sir!* ('Two and Two Makes Nun') and as Morris Coates in *The Fall and Rise of Reginald Perrin*. Film appearances include Dr Crippen in Marty Feldman's *The Last Remake of Beau Geste* and *A Fish Called Wanda* with John Cleese. From 1993, he enjoyed a year in Manchester as Bernard Morten in *Coronation Street*.

THE GOODIES
BEASTLY RECORD

Bradley's Records may have released the biggest hits from *The Goodies*, Island Records was responsible for the team's greatest album, but their return to vinyl was down to interest from Columbia Records. Bill wrote all the animal-based comedy songs on the album and although many of the tracks – including one of their finest recordings, 'Terrapins' – are of high standard, the vast majority were resurrected from the back catalogue of radio's *I'm Sorry I'll Read That Again*.

Although not featured on the album, 'M.I.C.K.E.Y. M.O.U.S.E.' was released as a single in May 1978 with the *Beastly Record* track, 'Funky Farm', on the reverse. The A-side was a fairly straight version of the classic Mickey Mouse Club theme song marking the fiftieth anniversary

of the world's best-loved mouse. Although fully endorsed by the Walt Disney Organisation, under the production of Miki Antony the team couldn't resist a bit of comic banter, explaining that Mickey isn't a 'hippapota-Mouse' or 'Anony-Mouse' but 'Fa-Mouse'! The trio performed the song on *Blue Peter* and tied in with a major BBC celebration of Mickey's milestone birthday. Sadly, the single didn't enter the British charts and Bill, for one, was 'not surprised! That bloody Mickey Mouse song! I love the mouse, don't get me wrong, but that record. Arghh! That was the height of our soppiness. I thought, "We have got to get out of doing this sort of stuff."'

The final single release from the album was a three-track collection that showcased Graeme's vocal prowess

THE GOODIES
BEASTLY RECORD

EMI

PATRICK MOORE
(1923–)

on 'A Man's Best Friend Is His Duck' and 'Taking My Oyster For Walkies'. 'They were fun to record, more fun than the live performances,' he remembers. Both were vintage Bill compositions, with the composer taking the lead vocals on the original reggae number, 'Rastashanty'. When the team prerecorded a rendition of 'A Man's Best Friend Is His Duck' for *Crackerjack*, the song was censored for the children's programme, with the phrase 'piss off' replaced with an energetic 'get stuffed'. On 6 December, the Goodies performed the censored version once again for the following day's edition of *Top of the Pops*. Despite this publicity, the single failed to chart.

The album also proved commercially unsuccessful, while the back cover of the release boasted the rather ominous credit: 'The Goodies are (at the time of recording)...'

The host of the BBC space programme *The Sky at Night* since 1957, Moore made his first appearance in *The Goodies* in the series four episode, 'Invasion of the Moon Creatures', warning the nation that people are turning into rabbits, while playing with his carrot. He returned for suitably starry cameos in 'Lighthouse Keeping Loonies', 'Goodies Rule – O.K', 'U-Friend or UFO?' and 'Punky Business', the script for which detailed that 'if he can't do it, see who we can get for a quick gag'.

Series 8, Episode 1

GOODIES AND POLITICS

First broadcast: Monday, 14 January 1980, 8.10 p.m.

With Bill on the left and Tim on the right, Graeme snatches a profit. An amazing election, which produces an uncomfortable coalition.

Although it had been tentatively agreed that seven scripts of *The Goodies* would be delivered by 3 January 1979, David Gower (of BBC contracts) was forced to send a reminder on 15 January. At this stage the contracts hadn't even been signed. It was a situation knowingly commented on by Roger Hancock when he wrote to Gower on 26 April 1979. 'Believe it or not, I can at last send you the agreement for the Goodies' next series, duly signed.' Now internally referred to as 'The Goodies 1979 series', it was still mooted as consisting of seven programmes.

Location filming had begun in autumn 1979, with studio dates fixed for November. However, with the decade they had ruled fast nearing its end, the BBC naturally included *The Goodies* in the compilation spectacular, 'The 70s Stop Here!' Hosted by Penelope Keith and literally the last BBC programme of the decade, it was broadcast on New Year's Eve from 10.40 p.m. until midnight. Within a fortnight *The Goodies* would return to the corporation and the *Radio*

'I'll tell you something swankpot.

When the Revolution comes we'll have

you up against the wall.'

'Promises. Promises!'

Left: Politics is a drag as Tim plays Margaret Thatcher and Bill plays Vanessa Redgrave.

Above: 'Timita' plans on emulating the Iron Lady's glamorous rise to the top!

Times preview signed off on the seventies show with the observation: 'The Goodies go on being good!'

The actual episode that brought *The Goodies* back to full strength after over two years away was a suitably biting satire on the rise and rise of recently elected Prime Minister Margaret Thatcher. The Iron Lady had come a long way since being sent up as an opposition puppet in 'Goodies Rule – O.K', with her story retold in terms of Andrew Lloyd Webber's *Evita*. Tim is the Conservative heroine Timita and delivers one of the most unforgettable of *Goodies* gags when he begs a couple of tearful secretaries (Maria Eldridge and Penny Irving), 'Don't cry for me, Marge and Tina'. Bill is the hairy, right-on Che Guevara figure, fighting on behalf of the Workers Revolutionary Party, while Graeme creams it in with his ad agency, Snaatchi and Snatchy. Again the comedy is heightened by the presence of a real BBC broadcaster in the shape of political commentator David Dimbleby as David Dimbleblm.

BLACK CINDERELLA II GOES EAST

Although the BBC had kept interest in *The Goodies* high with separate repeat seasons in February and September 1978 and an offer for a new series was on the table, it wasn't until Christmas that the team were reunited. Radio 2 presented 'Black Cinderella II Goes East or Confessions of a Glass Slipper Tryer Onner; the show that will do for pantomime what Mozart did for fluid mechanics'. The programme gathered together the classic *I'm Sorry I'll Read That Again* team (including John Cleese as the Fairy Godperson) with the Goodies as camp and bitchy Ugly Sisters. Producer Douglas Adams also attracted Peter Cook to the role of Prince Disgusting, Rob Buckman was Prince Charming and Liberal Member of Parliament, John Pardoe, played himself. Written by Rory McGrath and Clive Anderson, the *Radio Times* mockingly observed, 'The fact that everyone involved in this show is an ex-member of Cambridge Footlights is completely coincidental and has nothing to do with any form of nepotism or old boy network at all, whatsoever, honestly.'

NOEL EDMONDS PRESENTS MULTICOLOURED SWAP SHOP'S ROCK GARDEN PARTY

Regular *Swap Shop* host Noel Edmonds presented a live musical spectacular produced by Crispin Evans from a garden in Central London on Bank Holiday Monday, 29 May 1978. The Goodies joined fellow pop favourites, the Darts, Patti Boulaye and Showaddywaddy. Tim and Graeme wore *Unvarnished Truth* T-shirts as a plug for their stage venture.

SATURDAY NIGHT GREASE

First broadcast: Monday, 21 January 1980, 8.10 p.m.

The Goodies are into the disco scene, with Tim Travolta and Olivia Newton Grayboots, live from the Disco Bilius.

With *Saturday Night Fever*, *Grease* and *Staying Alive* the hot film musicals of the moment, Tim moves his affections from the Queen to Olivia Newton-John. Graeme makes a worrying sexy partner in tight black trousers and blonde wig. With No-Contact Discos all the rage, the Goodies endorse the perverse idea of a Mixed Disco Dancing Championship. Choreographer Flick Colby orchestrated a mini-history of dance as the trio escape the police via the Fred and Ginger Café, a *West Side*

Story routine, a bit of *Singin' in the Rain* and a *Wizard of Oz* finale. Bill's tribute to the faithful trandem, 'Grease Cycling', is a classic, but it was Tim that proudly 'got a complaint from Mary Whitehouse, which pleased us no end. She wrote to the Director General complaining that "Tim Brooke-Taylor was seen undressing, mocking John Travolta in an exceedingly tight pair of underpants with a distinctive carrot motif on the front..."' I'm just pleased she saw it.'

Bill fronts the 'Disco Bilius'.

Tim demonstrates the latest moves to his 'stunning' partner!

Tim 'plugging away' at his Travolta image.

Series 8, Episode 3

A KICK IN THE ARTS

First broadcast: Monday, 28 January 1980, 8.10 p.m.

It's the 1980 Olympics with the host nation Great Britain against the Rest of the World: Brooke-Taylor for GB, Garden and Oddie for RoW. The results – incredible.

With the Moscow Olympics just round the corner, the time was right for another discouraging comment on the state of British sport, with Hamlet Diving and Poetry Weight Lifting events stacked in their favour. Ballard Berkeley, having the previous year wrapped up his stint as *Fawlty Towers* resident Major Gowers, is the latest Goody face of government authority. And the notion of marrying world-class sportsmen to Virginia Wade and world-class sportswomen to Bill in order to make them British is an inspired one. It could even have led to Zola Budd, Greg Rusedski and Chelsea Football Club!

The Goodies get knitted for charity.

Series 8, Episode 4

U-FRIEND OR UFO?

First broadcast: Monday, 4 February 1980, 8.10 p.m.

There's something strange in the night sky. Bill has a close encounter, Graeme has electronic compulsions and Tim is moved by fear and liquid oxygen.

With *Star Wars*, *Close Encounters of the Third Kind* and *Alien* box-office hits, the Goodies grab a timely chance to send up Unidentified Flying Objects, with Graeme's mad scientist putting a nuclear warhead on Tim's head and launching him into space. Along the way, Graeme unveils a hybrid R2-D2 known as EBGB (Electronic Brain of Great Britain) and, hot on the heels of Tom Baker's defeat of them in *Doctor Who* ('Destiny of the Daleks'), a world-dominating pepper pot pops up with a cry of 'Exterminate!' Utilising the creations of George Lucas and Terry Nation, Graeme recalls, 'Oddly enough, we didn't need to get permission, as far as I know.'

Tim still suffering for his art on location in Dorset.

Series 8, Episode 5

ANIMALS

First broadcast: Monday, 11 February 1980, 8.10 p.m.

Tim runs an agency for animal actors, so Bill and Graeme force them to work in solving the energy crisis. But wronged animals discover their rights and stage a revolution.

Tim's agency can't even provide lions for Captain Grayboots the Fearless Lion Tamer and the latest BBC wildlife show is 'Life On Presenters'. Graeme, adopting the hushed tones of David Attenborough, searches for everything from the fossilised remains of Michaela and Armand Denis to a destructive family of David Bellamys. Referencing *Watership Down*, the trio end up as ill-fated rabbits and see their own show usurped by an animal substitute ... 'The Doggies'.

And contemporary comedy is embraced, with *Not the Nine O'Clock News* star Mel Smith making a cameo appearance as a 'Not the News At Ten' newscaster.

Tim and Bill fail to see the funny side of life as doomed bunnies.

Series 8, Episode 6

WAR BABIES

First broadcast: Monday, 18 February 1980, 8.10 p.m.

1940 STOP BRITAIN BESIEGED STOP HOW DID CHURCHILL WIN THE WAR QUERY ONLY NOW CAN IT BE TOLD STOP AND ONLY THREE SMALL BOYS CAN TELL IT SEMI COLON REUTERS

Broadcast on Graeme's thirty-seventh birthday, this would prove to be the very last episode of *The Goodies* on BBC television. The war years, in which they were born, are conjured up with sepia newsreel footage, 1940s music and even a burst of the *Dad's Army* theme. It's a truly fictional account of how the team meet at the special school, Highbrow Hall, under the watchful eye of the Headmaster (Geoffrey Palmer) and the sexy Matron (Sharon Miller). Andrew Ray provides a telling cameo as Winston Churchill, who is forced to stay in hiding because he looks like Adolf Hitler! Tim, disguised as Churchill, wins the day by beating Germany at football. Churchill gets a knighthood, and the Goodies get lollipops!

What the Goodies were expecting, though, was at least the seventh episode that had been commissioned in 1978. The six episodes of series eight plus 'Bunfight at the O.K. Tearooms' were repeated in October and November 1980 while the team were on stand-by and continually losing hope for a proposed Christmas Special that never came. 'That annoyed us,' says Bill. 'As far as I was concerned the BBC could go and get stuffed after that. I love them again now, of course!'

You Don't Want To Do It Alone.

CHANNEL CROSSING

'I have always said that leaving the BBC was the biggest mistake we ever made!' claims Tim. 'I really believe that. It was pressure from Bill and Graeme that finally decided it.'

Bill explains, 'All I know was that they told us the budget couldn't be spared for *The Goodies*. It was a very expensive show to make and it seemed our budget was being used for *The Hitchhiker's Guide to the Galaxy*. That was fine. Douglas Adams was a fellow Cambridge Footlights member. Good luck to him. I just couldn't understand why the BBC couldn't do both shows. It wasn't as though Doug's programme was anything like what we were doing. But the BBC made an either/or choice and we lost out.'

It's Nearly The End So Quick Find a Friend

Dummies! A new challenge for the old team during the making of 'Change of Life'.

'It was thought that the BBC were trying out *The Hitchhiker's Guide to the Galaxy* and were planning a sequel later in the year,' remembers Graeme. 'Basically they just told us to wait. If the *Hitchhiker's* show was a complete disaster they would want us back for another series. I just felt quite cross about that. We were being treated like second-class citizens. And this was after doing the show for ten, very successful, years. I just thought we deserved better, quite frankly.'

Tim also recalls that both Bill and Graeme 'had just been going through rather messy, very expensive divorces and I think they wanted to take the first offer that came along.'

That offer came from the other side: commercial television. 'David Bell from London Weekend Television approached us,' recalls Bill. 'He said, "I think it's time you came and worked for us!" He was the executive producer on our ITV series. Now, don't forget the BBC hadn't made

us an offer for another series. Our Christmas show had been dropped and that was that.'

According to Graeme, 'It seemed the BBC were not in love with us any more. Both Bill and I were very happy to accept the offer from LWT.'

The offer was a particularly attractive one. 'It was like being let loose in a sweet shop,' enthuses Bill. 'They promised us a film project, a three-year deal and double the budget the BBC had given us for our last series. And personally we were getting paid a ridiculous amount. Ridiculous, but fully justified, of course! But it was almost as much as we had earned from ten years with the BBC.'

Tim was still reluctant to make the move, but finally bowed to the judgement of Bill and Graeme. 'I accepted the *Hitchhiker's* excuse,' says Tim, 'but there were other, lamer excuses which stretched the point a bit. Eventually the BBC delayed one more time and I gave way. And LWT seemed very eager to have us. I just hoped it would be the same as before.'

'We just didn't feel welcome at the BBC any more,' says Bill. 'It wasn't just the *Hitchhiker's* thing. Maybe someone high up just thought it was more trouble than it was worth having us about the place. Perhaps we were considered old hat. *Not the Nine O'Clock News* was on. The peerless Rik Mayall and the rest were coming up. This was the new face of comedy. It was. Fair enough. But did that mean the old-timers had to be put out to graze? Obviously it did, because we were put out to graze. And pretty much wiped from the memory as far as BBC comedy was concerned.'

A move to LWT was just the refreshing change the Goodies needed. Promised a 'created by Tim Brooke-Taylor, Graeme Garden and Bill Oddie' credit on all programmes, the team was also given the luxury of time. The first four shows of the series were in the studio as early as May and June 1981, with the final two recorded in October. And for Bill and Graeme as writers it was one of their most prolific times. Not only were they writing the new *Goodies* shows, but also a science-fiction sitcom for ITV, *Astronauts*.

'I think it was my idea and I pitched it to Bill,' says Graeme. 'It struck me as the one brand new realistic situation for a sitcom: the comedy of claustrophobia like *Steptoe*, or more closely *Porridge*. So we pitched it to Dick Clement and Ian Le Fresnais, who were very enthusiastic, and their company made the series. I think it probably fell between several stools: we tried to make it realistic, but that didn't really suit our style that well, and people weren't familiar enough with the situation. We should have hung on a few years and done *Red Dwarf*.'

As Bill told the *TV Times* in January 1982, 'Last year we sometimes weren't sure which we were writing.' Although the new *Goodies* series had been in the studio from May 1981, their launch on the new channel was with a Christmas special. As promised, they had been rewarded with a film project, albeit only a twenty-five-minute one.

THE GOODIES GREATEST HITS

With the Goodies preparing to relaunch themselves on ITV, the back catalogue of Bradley's Records and Columbia *Goodies* classics were brought together for this twenty-track collection from EMI. A valuable record of the Goodies as pop stars, the disc also featured the album debut of 'M.I.C.K.E.Y. M.O.U.S.E.' The new series was heralded with a cover shot of the team from 'Big Foot'.

The ultimate Goody pop package from 1981.

THIS IS YOUR LIFE

Tim was the subject of a 1981 edition of the show hosted by Eamonn Andrews. 'I was asked to go and do a radio commercial at a hotel near Shepherds Bush. I asked, why not do it at a recording studio. I was told it would sound more authentic on location. I was a bit puzzled, but didn't really think too much about it. As I was going up an escalator in the hotel I noticed lots of people I knew coming down the other escalator. My thoughts were, "There seems to have been a jolly party that I wasn't invited to. Damn."'

In 2000, Michael Aspel stung Bill during the filming of a nature programme for the BBC. Having vowed never to take part in the show, he reluctantly went through the experience and greeted Tim and Graeme sporting Ecky-Thump caps at the start of the recording. 'Graeme hasn't been "done" yet,' says Tim ominously.

Eamonn Andrews presents Tim with the Big Red Book in February 1981.

The Goodies Christmas Special

SNOW WHITE 2

First broadcast: Sunday, 27 December 1981, 7.15 p.m.

Just when you thought it was safe to go back to the pantomime . . .

In the late 1970s the Goodies had toyed with the idea of staging a pantomime made up of all the traditional elements. The idea came to naught, but it was resurrected here with a saucy Snow White (Annette Lyons), the Goodies as Buttons, a pantomime cow – 'it was amazingly hot inside her!' said Bill – knowing narration from Richard Briers and eleven wicked princesses. 'Why eleven wicked princesses? Because we couldn't afford to recruit a couple of hundred!' explained Bill.

But best of all were the dwarfs. Twelve actors were on call to play the seven friends of Snow White. 'We had been writing roles for vertically challenged actors for years,' says Bill, 'ever since we did a mini cops thing for *Twice A Fortnight* which had five little policemen in a little police car. Bob Spiers got very embarrassed. On the "Snow White" show he would say, "Can we have the um … little … um … short … um." "It's all right," said one, "you can call us what we are." "OK," said Bob, "can we have the dwarfs here?" "We're not dwarfs!" "Oh, sorry!"'

Talking to the *TV Times*, Spiers reflected, 'It's a complex story', and pitied one of his dwarf actors when a goldfish, 'a big one, comes up and swallows him. He was a very brave, poor little soul being eaten by a goldfish, especially as he wanted to go to the loo at the time.' 'Snow White 2' was compared to *Jaws 2* by Spiers, while the *Star Wars*-like laser wand of Tim's Fairy Timbalina was 'absolutely deliberate'.

And while the slapstick and subject matter was aimed at the younger audience, there was still plenty of adult undertones to the humour. Used as the prelude

to the trio's ITV series, the special was in fact the very last *Goodies* episode recorded. Filmed over a nine-day schedule, it was in the studio on 9 December 1981, just two weeks before its broadcast.

Over-sized dwarfs on location. The Goodies embrace pantomime traditions.

Series 9, Episode 1

ROBOT

First broadcast: Saturday, 9 January 1982, 6.45 p.m.

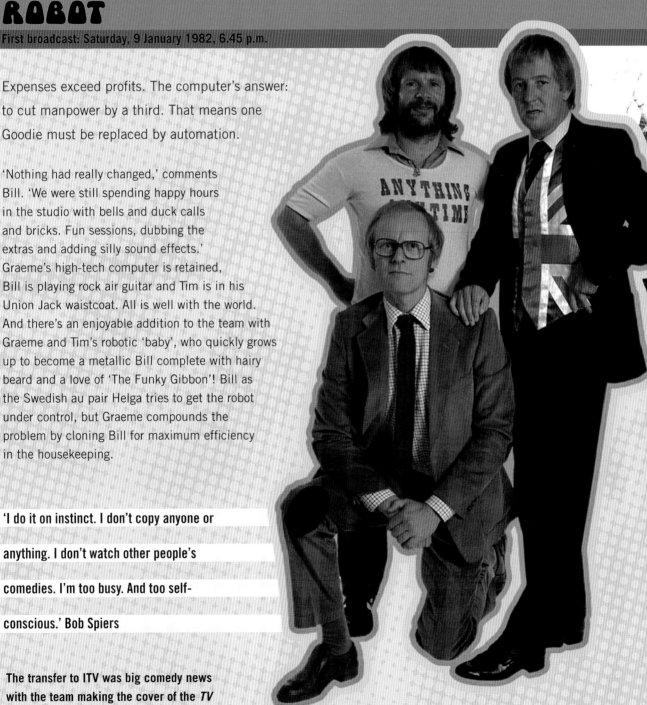

Expenses exceed profits. The computer's answer: to cut manpower by a third. That means one Goodie must be replaced by automation.

'Nothing had really changed,' comments Bill. 'We were still spending happy hours in the studio with bells and duck calls and bricks. Fun sessions, dubbing the extras and adding silly sound effects.' Graeme's high-tech computer is retained, Bill is playing rock air guitar and Tim is in his Union Jack waistcoat. All is well with the world. And there's an enjoyable addition to the team with Graeme and Tim's robotic 'baby', who quickly grows up to become a metallic Bill complete with hairy beard and a love of 'The Funky Gibbon'! Bill as the Swedish au pair Helga tries to get the robot under control, but Graeme compounds the problem by cloning Bill for maximum efficiency in the housekeeping.

'I do it on instinct. I don't copy anyone or anything. I don't watch other people's comedies. I'm too busy. And too self-conscious.' Bob Spiers

The transfer to ITV was big comedy news with the team making the cover of the *TV Times* in January 1982.

Series 9, Episode 2

FOOTBALL CRAZY

First broadcast: Saturday, 16 January 1982, 6.45 p.m.

A bearded hooligan causes trouble on the football terraces. Tim elects to stamp it out himself.

What ensues is a cross-fertilisation between the football hooliganism of Bill and the balletic style of Graeme, who contributes an impressively limp dying swan to the finale. Guest stars are gleaned from both cultural camps, with legendary 1966 World Cup commentator Kenneth Wolstenholme interviewing Bill's crew-cut yob, and ballet dancer Wayne Sleep throwing himself into the ballet melee. But it's Tim who puts himself forward as the law enforcer, attempting to cut down on football violence by insisting that only one fan can attend each match!

A Polaroid snap of Tim and Bill between takes; and Bill, as Helga the Au Pair, cuddles up to the robot!

'Strictly Dance Fever' with ballet star Wayne Sleep showing Bill and Graeme how it's done!

DAVID RAPPAPORT

(1951–90)

Britain's best-loved dwarf actor, Rappaport first came to comic notice as Little Dave in Spike Milligan's *Q* series, later appearing as Shades in *Tiswas* and in *The Young Ones* ('Boring' and 'Flood'). He hit the big time in films as Randall the leader of the Time Bandits in the film of the same name and Rinaldo in *The Bride*, finding success on American television as Hamilton Skylar in *LA Law* and Simon in *The Wizard*. Having provided the cheeky vocals for the Goodies metal adversary in 'Robot' and 'Change of Life', he proved so popular with the team that he was invited back to appear in the flesh as the lead dwarf in 'Snow White 2'.

'We [the Goodies] had replaced three of the dwarfs,' says Bill, 'and David looked us up and down and had this great line... "It has come to my attention that some of you are not dwarfs!" He was hilarious.'

A dapper-looking David Rappaport.

Series 9, Episode 3

BIG FOOT

First broadcast: Saturday, 23 January 1982, 6.45 p.m.

Arthur C. Clarke – man or myth? Intrigued by this dilemma, the Goodies investigate. Their journey eventually leads to the Canadian Rockies, where they tangle with the legendary Big Foot.

In actual fact, Graeme is Arthur C. Clarke all along, gamely going on with his broadcast while alien space travellers fill up at Stonehenge and the Loch Ness Monster looks over his shoulder. But he doesn't want to disappoint Tim and Bill, so he joins his fellow Goodies in the search for Clarke. He even adds to the mystery by tossing up dinner plates to suggest UFOs and even letting his wig slip for a quick glimpse of the Clarke persona underneath!

Tim's sleepwalking round the mountain gives him one leg shorter than the other, there's Bill and Graeme dancing while disguised as bears and, eventually, all three Goodies get the Big Foot look!

Big Foot Fever!

Series 9, Episode 4

CHANGE OF LIFE

First broadcast: Saturday, 30 January 1982, 6.45 p.m.

It's Bill's birthday. Tim and Graeme decide to celebrate on a grand scale, but Bill doesn't want to know. Lethargy sets in and all efforts to recapture their lost youth fail.

Facing the thought of being forty, Bill drags his fellow Goodies down and the team face the fact that they may well be too old to be Goodies. Helped by Bill's song, 'You're Only As Old As You Feel', performed by Bones, a trio of grannies wears them out and they face their biggest challenge, The Goodies Standard Test. Can the team cut it like they used to? All the old favourites are resurrected, with a half-hearted performance of 'The Funky Gibbon', Kitten Kong, an ecky-thump robot complete with cloth cap, the dam-busting geese, a Nicholas Parsons attack and even a five-point deduction because of Tim's overacting. 'It's a little close for comfort, all that,' smiles Tim. 'Perhaps we were subconsciously admitting that we were a bit too old for all that silly stuff.'

As for Bill, he grew rather attached to Tim's Goody stand-in dummy, slumping him over his drum kit at home and telling the *TV Times* in 1982, 'He's been here for about three weeks. People nearly have heart attacks. We were covered in plaster of Paris from the neck up, with straws up our nostrils for breathing. It wasn't pleasant, particularly for me with my beard. Graeme and I had to do a charity show the other week and Tim couldn't make it, so we managed with that gentleman there. I never talk to him. I talk to the real Tim.'

Time to call it a day? The Goodies face the fact that age is catching up with them.

Series 9, Episode 5

HOLIDAY

First broadcast: Saturday, 6 February 1982, 6.45 p.m.

Relationships are strained when Tim is left at home to do the housework, while Bill and Graeme go out to work. A sunshine holiday at Dunsquabblin is Tim's solution.

Bill and Graeme indulge in a spot of Victoriana.

In a return to the single-set format of classics like 'The End' and 'Earthanasia', the team pass the time during a rain-sodden holiday. The fall guy is Bill, with the other two picking on him, mocking him because he has no friends to send postcards to, throwing tea over him and even bashing him with mallets. 'I used to lie awake at night worrying about a show where Tim and Graeme had the chance to hurt me,' says Bill. 'They used to relish the opportunity for revenge far too much!'

Still, Tim does indulge his hairy friend with a spot of indoor bird-watching by impersonating some feathered friends: he blows out his cheeks for a puffin and gets his zip stuck for a flycatcher! The episode closes with a punk rock version of 'I Do Like to Be Beside the Seaside'. 'I cadged a Yamaha drum kit for that scene,' says Bill. 'I remember two guys from the company came to the recording and were horrified at what I was doing to their equipment!'

Series 9, Episode 6

ANIMALS ARE PEOPLE TOO

First broadcast: Saturday, 13 February 1982, 6.45 p.m.

Graybags Pet Shop is clean out of pets. To help with the unemployment problem, Graeme decides to stock people-pets. Tim, his first customer, is delighted by the purchase of a lovable little scamp called Bill.

Tim is inspired by celebrated dog trainer Barbara Woodhouse and puts his very human dog through his paces, although little Bill still continues to get into bed with his owner! Graeme's Rumbling Tum restaurant satisfies Tim's hunger, although he's shocked to discover that the hamster burgers and gerbil dumplings aren't just gimmick menu names. But with animals in short supply Graeme starts fattening up humans for food. Bill and Tim tuck into a huge pie, but when they

Tim trains Bill 'the Woodhouse Way'.

discover Graeme's glasses, alarm bells ring. Fortunately the mad scientist is safe and well in a kennel bearing the legend: 'Beware of the Loony'.

With a Warner Brothers cartoon-styled 'That's All Folks!' the episode, the series and *The Goodies* came to an end. 'It just seemed a fitting way to sign off a very animal-based cartoony episode,' says Graeme. 'We didn't know it was the last ever.'

Having recorded the series before the Christmas special, the writing was quickly on the wall in 1982 when managing director Michael Grade dropped *The Goodies* after the first year of their three-year contract. The official reason was that the programme was too expensive. 'But we hadn't asked for the increased budget,' complains Bill. 'That was what we were offered. Perhaps if we had had more of a say in how the show was made we could have made it a lot cheaper. Who knows? But it certainly wasn't down to us. Obviously LWT lost faith in the show.'

Graeme maintains, 'ITV costings were different to the BBC's, and the costs turned out to be much higher than anticipated.'

'They really didn't know where to put us in the schedules,' says Tim. 'It was criminal, really.'

'We would have liked to go out at nine o'clock or a little later,' adds Bill. 'But I suppose they saw us as family entertainers. People were still watching. The first episode of the series got the highest ratings we had ever had. But the audience didn't stay. It was a big mistake.'

'I resisted saying "I told you so",' says Tim, 'but I did tell them! I was very upset about it.'

'Naturally it was upsetting,' continues Graeme, 'especially after we had been promised a three-year contract and had planned for that. But I suppose it was cheaper to pay us off and let us go than to actually make the programmes at what it was costing them.'

Bill remains confident that 'we could have gone on for years and years'.

Tim is even more ebullient. 'We would still be running today. Like *Last of the Summer Wine*!'

BOB SPIERS
(1945 –)

As a production assistant for David Croft, Spiers worked on such hit sitcoms as *Dad's Army* and *Are You Being Served?* before graduating to director for *It Ain't Half Hot, Mum* and *Come Back Mrs Noah!* In 1979 he directed the first series of *Not the Nine O'Clock News* and the last series of *Fawlty Towers*. Between 1977 and 1981 he directed all nineteen episodes of *The Goodies*.

'Bob came into the picture quite late on and added an extra dimension,' remembers Tim. 'We had all got a bit stuck in our ways and Bob helped by being a bit more ambitious in the look of the shows. Some of his work, especially at LWT, was a triumph.'

Later comedy credits have included *The Comic Strip*, *Murder Most Horrid*, *Absolutely Fabulous*, *Bottom* and *Ant and Dec's Tribute to The Likely Lads*. He also directed the all-star musical romp *Spice World: the Movie* as well as the 1997 Walt Disney remake of *That Darn Cat*.

Contemporary Ways Are Driving Me Crazy…

TAKE ME BACK

'**W**e were never given that opportunity to say goodbye to *The Goodies*,' complains Bill. 'We didn't say, "Right, that's it. Let's call it a day." As a result we have remained Goodies ever since. And it's been a bloody long time!'

At the start of 1983 the team were already reuniting on a regular basis. 'We never really split up. That was the thing,' explains Graeme. 'As a result we were asked to do bits and pieces on programmes and public appearances as a group, even though the only thing keeping us together as a group were those very programmes and public appearances.'

The first of these commitments was a charity concert organised by Adrian Slade and performed at the Theatre Royal on 21 January. Tim's 'discovery', Humphrey Barclay, directed 'An Evening At Court', which recruited the cream of British comedy including Peter Cook, John Cleese, Rowan Atkinson,

Eleanor Bron, David Frost, Dawn French and Jennifer Saunders. 'Humphrey got us involved,' says Graeme. 'I expect I did "Pets' Corner"!'

If the concert wasn't nostalgic enough, BBC1 commissioned a documentary dedicated to the history of the Cambridge Footlights. 'Footlight: 100 Years of Comedy' was broadcast on 4 June and featured interviews with such major players as Peter Cook, John Cleese, Tim, Graeme and Bill.

And despite obvious tensions between the BBC and the

Goodies, the first wave of home-video releases for classic television in 1983 included the 1973 special 'The Goodies and the Beanstalk'. 'It wasn't a big seller for some reason,' says Bill. 'Oh, I know the reason! They were charging nearly sixty quid for it! Now I'm not saying forty-five minutes of *The Goodies* isn't worth nearly sixty quid. Of course it is! But it was a lot of money. The Great British Public could obviously quite happily live without it! Then I suppose someone at the BBC filed a memo saying 'Goodies videos do not sell',

Goodies fans were 'spoiled' with a whole fifty minutes of ITV fun on this 1986 video release.

because that was it for years and years. Mind you, someone told me that every single one of those expensive BBC videos were a little later re-released at a much cheaper price. Every one except one. Yes, you guessed it, *The Goodies*. That wasn't released again until years and years later. I sense a pattern emerging!'

Still, the Goodies were signed up to provide the vocal talent for a new cartoon series from producer Trevor Bond and director Terry Ward. Bananaman was a rather slow-witted, endearing superhero who had first appeared within the pages of *Monster Fun* comic in the early 1970s. Graeme provided the earnest, slightly bewildered voice for the star of the show, while Tim's patriotic narration held the plots together. He was also the voice of Eric, 'the schoolboy who leads an exciting double life, for when Eric eats a banana an amazing transformation occurs – Eric is Bananaman, ever alert for the call to action!'

Bill's major character was a friendly black crow that accompanied Bananaman on his misadventures, throwing in corny gags at every opportunity. The supporting gallery of grotesques was dished out to the trio fairly evenly, with Bill as Chief O'Reilly and the monosyllabic slimeball King Zorg, leader of the Nerks. Tim excelled as the evil Appleman from the West Country and the Peter Lorre-styled Dr Doom. Graeme provided himself with his own arch-villain, Colonel Blight. For Tim it was 'enormous fun. Who could resist playing cartoon characters? Originally I was meant to play Bananaman and Eric, but Graeme's mastery of the Bananaman voice was too good to pass over.'

The series was a huge success, running almost continually through the 1980s and remaining a staple repeat favourite to this day. And talking of repeats, even the BBC had been re-running old episodes of *The Goodies* in 1984. It wasn't much, but three classic programmes from the final BBC series were aired in January. ITV repeated their collection of episodes from June 1984. It marked the last regular terrestrial exposure for the series. Two video releases from the ITV archives were also released.

'**Bananaman' and the Goodies chat to *Blue Peter* presenter Janet Ellis in 1983.**

The BBC still seemed keen on the format if not on the original show. Graeme and Bill were approached with regard to adapting some vintage scripts for a children's series tentatively entitled 'The New Goodies'. 'My first reaction was a raised eyebrow!' chuckles Bill. 'Graeme and I discussed it ,but in all honesty we both felt that if it was going to be done at all it should be done well. And to do it well would have cost an awful lot of money. I thought it might all turn out looking a bit sad as well. It was going to be Phillip Schofield or some of his broom-cupboard chums running around doing our old stuff. It makes me shiver just to think about it!'

The BBC clearly weren't that married to the idea or, if they were, they weren't about to start reusing old props, for, in 1984, the Goodies trandem was put up for auction. Hugh Spowers bought it and, alongside his brother Rory and occasionally Bill Oddie, the bike was used in several charity events. 'It was amazing to me how popular this bloody trandem had become! It got more attention than I did for a start, and even when we tour Australia it's the first thing people ask us. "Where's the bike, mate?" They couldn't care less if we were there or not!'

Back in Britain it was still slim pickings for *Goodies* fans as the 1980s rolled on. In November 1986 the BBC repeated 'Kitten Kong' as part of its massive retrospective season, 'TV50', but it wasn't until 1988 that fans were excited by a rumour that the team were set to reunite for *Comic Relief*.

Doctors Alan Maryon, Gillian Rice and Graeme Garden present *Body Matters*: 'What A Mouthful!' in July 1986.

Indeed they did reunite, but only for a brief, prefilmed contribution to a quick-fire sketch collection entitled '73 of a Kind'. 'Maybe someone at the BBC thought we were only worth bringing back together for two-and-a-half minutes!' comments Bill, 'but I think it proved one thing. We were still funny, I hope, and we still worked really well together. I'm furiously passionate about this. Whatever happens, whatever time we are given, Tim and Graeme and I make a good team. There, I've said it!'

The central conceit of their appearance on *Comic Relief* is that each Goodie has received a letter of invitation. Typically Graeme's name is spelled wrong and the 'very, very, very young' producers of *Comic Relief* have decided that 'in preparing our star-studded bill of wit, humour, fun and frolics it has been suggested that we include something by the Goodies. To provide a bit of contrast!'

Bill takes up the letter. 'We are very much aware that people remember *The Goodies* with the same nostalgic affection that they remember ration books, hoo-la hoops and Wolverhampton Wanderers!' The letter infers knowledge that the trio had a hit record with 'The Funky Gilbert' and ponders, 'We thought you might like to recreate that. So we got it out of the archives and played it and then we thought perhaps you wouldn't like to recreate it after all. But don't

worry, it's for charity, so it doesn't have to be very good!' The embittered Goodies screw up their letters and eagerly introduce 'The Funky GIBBON' with a hand-clapping jive and a rousing 'Do, do, do the Funky...' before the BBC pull the plug and bring the performance to an end.

Hilariously self-deprecating, it's tinged with the awareness that the Goodies were fast becoming relics. 'We are also aware, of course,' the letter continues, 'that today one of you is a doctor, one of you is a bird-watcher and one of you has left the entertainment business entirely!'

Graeme was always a doctor, but since 1985 had been hosting the BBC1 medical series, *Body Matters*. Alongside fellow doctors Alan Maryon and Gillian Rice, Graeme looked at every aspect of the body under such inviting, humorous titles as 'On Your Knees', 'You've Got A Nerve!' and 'Gut Feelings'.

Bill was always a bird-watcher, but his hobby had started to become his career with the bestselling *Bill Oddie's Little Black Bird Book*, a 1985 *Nature Watch* programme ('Bill Oddie – Bird-Watcher') and 1986's *Bird Week*.

And Tim, of course, had never left the entertainment business. It was just a mockery of his safe and cosy encampment in the realms of television situation comedy. At the time he was still playing Richard O'Sullivan's gullible

School Reunion. Back together again to promote their 1993 *Billy Bunter* radio series.

friend, Derek Yates, in the ITV sitcom *Me and My Girl*. And, from September 1987, he had been starring as Tom Hammond opposite Diane Keen's successful novelist in the BBC1 series *You Must Be the Husband*. 'I enjoyed that. Colin Bostock-Smith is a great writer. I get annoyed when people said, "Ooh, it's a cosy sofa sitcom!" I say, "Yeah! So's *Frasier*. So's *Hancock*. So's *Steptoe and Son*. So's *Only Fools and Horses*." It's good stuff. There's a sofa in it because most people tend to have a sofa in their sitting room!'

Still, Graeme and Bill couldn't resist another bash at Tim's sitcom success when the trio reunited again, along with John Cleese, Jo Kendall and David Hatch, for the 25th-anniversary special of *I'm Sorry I'll Read That Again*. Broadcast on Radio 2 on Christmas Day 1989, the second half of this hour-long show resurrected the 'Jack the Ripper' spoof from the last series, back in 1973. However, the first half intriguingly saw the cast tracked down to their current whereabouts. Tim has again seemingly left comedy behind him. Bill remembers, 'We did ten years of *The Goodies* with him, he gave it up just before that!' Now a resident of Milton Sitcom, where vicars and bosses are always unexpectedly dropping round for tea and every entrance must start with a cheery "Hello darling, I'm home", Tim is saved from his plight and rejoins his old team-mates.

By the time of the broadcast John Cleese was weary of reunions. He had contributed to a glut of twentieth-anniversary tributes to *Monty Python*, all of them dampened by the death of Graham Chapman in October 1989. His joyous memorial service saw Tim and Bill join in with the final 'hymn': 'Always Look on the Bright Side of Life'.

But 1990, the twentieth anniversary of *The Goodies*, saw no such retrospective. Indeed, the team wasn't back in action until 1993 and then it was for another 'unofficial' reunion. A pet project of Bill's, *The Billy Bunter Stories*, proved a popular addition to Radio 2's output. Six programmes were broadcast from July, with Bill bagging the lead role of Frank Richard's immortal 'fat owl' of Greyfriars school, 'because it was my idea!' Graeme's favourite contribution came with

his steely performance as the unforgiving tutor Mr Quelch. Tim provided the narration – 'by default', according to Bill, 'because there was nothing else for him to do!' In actual fact, Tim supplemented his cheery commentary with several supporting roles, most notably that of the raffish charmer Bob Cherry.

Finally, in 1994, BBC Video announced that the Goodies had been asked to select their six favourite episodes for a commercial release. 'We were sent every single episode and told to go through and pick the best ones,' groans Bill. 'I'm sure Tim did that, but for me it was obvious. We had to have the beanstalk. We had to have "Kitten Kong". We had

Diane Keen's saucy book shocks Tim in the sitcom, *You Must Be the Husband*.

to have the squeezy tomato gunfight. All the ones people remembered, really. Actually, I did watch some of the tapes and realised just how bad some of the shows were! They were terrible. To be fair, the BBC did take notice of what we said. I was worried that a load of rubbish would be put out!'

But the trio found the promotion of the tapes unsatisfactory. 'The people involved were very good but the distribution and the advertising was practically nonexistent,' continues Bill. 'It used to be called BBC Enterprises – there's a contradiction in terms if ever there was one! We asked them, "Why aren't you advertising the tapes?" and they would say they "only spent time and money on tapes if the programmes were actually being broadcast on television"! Well, show them on television, then! It was hopeless! I mean we did the odd radio and magazine interview, posed with the bloody trandem and everything, but the BBC just didn't seem to know how to market the tapes.'

Indeed, the press release happily kept the series stuck in the 1970s, instructing would-be purchasers to 'dig out your flares and turn back the clock with the return of *The Goodies*'. 'That really annoyed me,' moans Tim. 'We weren't just a funny show of the 1970s. We were a funny show full stop!'

'Although we were of the seventies,' admits Bill, 'it was only inasmuch as we ran on the BBC for the whole of that decade. I can imagine kids picking up the videos and thinking, "Who are these old farts?" and putting them back.'

'You have the BBC, with the best free advertising space in the country,' explains Tim. 'You show an episode of *The Goodies*. You hope people like it. Then, when it's finished, you tell them that you can go out and buy some more of the same on BBC video.'

'It happens all the time,' agrees Bill, 'but not with *The Goodies*!'

Bill was happier with the treatment his back catalogue of *Goodies* songs received from Music Club. A twenty-track compilation of greatest hits was released in March 1997 as

Graeme battled Jeremy Hardy in the political comedy panel show, *If I Ruled the World* in 1998. Clive Anderson was in the chair.

Yum Yum! The Very Best of the Goodies. 'The truth is that this is not a collection of *Goodies* songs,' said Bill at the time. 'These are my songs. Listening to them you're hearing a large part of my life. Sad isn't it? That they have been unavailable for so long, I mean.'

Bill took on several promotional appearances, including the ITV programme *Funny Business* and Virgin Radio's *Russ and Jono Show*, which featured an impromptu sing-along session with 'The Funky Gibbon' recording. 'For my own part,' he explained, 'the very existence of this collection is satisfaction enough. I ask for no further reward. Except perhaps for an interview in *Q*. Or maybe a Brit Award for Lifetime Achievement. Or perhaps to be voted Wanker of the Week on the Girlie Show. Failing that, how about some royalties?'

Still, royalties were certainly coming at a steady trickle from down under. 'We were still massive in Australia,' says Tim, 'and Bill's songs had been taken to the nation's heart.' Spiderbait had recorded a version of 'Run' for their 1992 debut album, *Shasahvaglava*. Melbourne-based group Plastic Spaceman had even named themselves after a *Goodies* commercial from 'Radio Goodies' and punctuated their album, *Exhibit A*, with extracts from the series. Another Australian band, Feverdream, included more sound bites from the show on a slowed-down rendition of 'The Goodies Theme' that was featured on their 1995 album *Moniker*.

The Goodies reunited for a programme for the Australian station, Channel 7. 'Where Are They Now?' was broadcast on 14 November 1997 and, according to Bill, '... ended up being more like "Who the fuck were you anyway?"' Still, it opened the floodgates. The team was back in demand.

And it wasn't just in Australia. Tim recalls, 'My son Edward was in a band at university and he asked whether we would mind them performing the *Goodies* theme as part of their act. It was that whole drug-culture thing that appealed to him; as in Good Es, it's whatever turns you on! Would we mind? Of course not!'

Maybe it was the time when kids who had loved the show were finally becoming the media movers and shakers, or maybe it was just the right time to remember the show: for whatever reason, *The Goodies* were cool. On *The Harry Hill Show* Billy Bragg was invited to perform 'The Funky Gibbon'. Peter Kay observed that every contestant in old game shows looked like the Goodies. *TV Zone* magazine included Kitten Kong on the Post Office Tower in their '100 Best TV Moments of All Time', *Loaded* magazine included the Goodies in their ongoing 'Greatest Living Englishmen' section and Spice Girl Geri Halliwell openly adopted Tim's Union Jack dress sense for the Brit Awards. 'About one per cent of the royalties would shut me up!' he joked.

They reunited for Nick Setchfield's 'Goodiefellas' interview for April 1998's issue of *Cult TV* magazine, while in August the Goodies were interviewed by Gaby Roslin on BBC1's

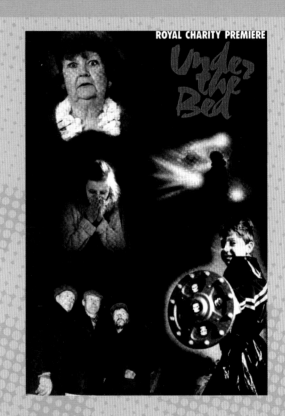

UNDER THE BED

Nicola Stewart and Thomas Arnold starred as siblings Felicity and George Piper in this 1988 film from the Children's Film Foundation. Directed by Colin Finbow and scripted by Laura Beaumont it told the tale of a monster created from rubbish kicked under the bed. Our junior crusaders must fight it. In their first big-screen appearance together all three Goodies reunited to lend stellar support as the dustbinmen.

PAUL FARRAH
presents

TIM BROOKE-TAYLOR SUSAN PENHALIGON TRACEY CHILDS

and

CARMEN SILVERA

in
STANLEY PRICE's
WEST END COMEDY HIT

WHY ME?

with
DAVID CARDY
& TOBY WALTON

Directed by
ROGER REDFARN

Designed by
JULIE GODFREY

Lighting by
LEONARD TUCKER

Associate Producer
IAN FRICKER

A Churchill Theatre Bromley/
Yvonne Arnaud Theatre
Guildford production

Mon 4 - Sat 9 September 2000
BOX OFFICE 01494 512000

WYCOMBE SWAN

METRO

Eves: Monday - Saturday 8.00pm. Mats: Wednesday & Saturday 2.30pm.

PFP

Tim's sitcom stardom keeps him a firm favourite in farce around the world … and in High Wycombe!

Television's Greatest Hits. 'Again, it was all of two-and-a-half minutes,' moans Bill. 'Those things are always the same. We get the big build-up. They show lots of clips from *The Goodies*. Usually the giant kitten! And then we come on. By the time we say who we are we have to get off. I seem to remember Tim and Graeme being rather cross with me after that show. I was probably being a bit grouchy. But they actually wanted the show to be kept back in case it affected our image. Absolute nonsense. They did a radio show a little later, *In Conversation*, and friends of mine thought I had been snubbed. But I hadn't. They talked about *The Goodies*, of course, but it was mainly about *I'm Sorry I Haven't A Clue* and I was well out of that by that stage.'

With the rise and rise of cable television, old shows were the lifeblood of such nostalgia channels as UK Gold. *The Goodies*, often sliced and diced to fit the scheduling, was no exception. However, UK Arena were planning something rather more special. 'An Evening with the Goodies' was announced for 11 July 1998, showcasing three classic episodes and a new documentary, 'You Never Had it So Goodie'. But disagreements within the group saw this programme go unmade and the limited repeat season fared badly against that summer's football World Cup coverage.

Similarly in 1999, when the Goodies were invited to re-form for a special comedy show to mark the millennium, the trio declined. Tim explained, 'I think we all thought people would be expecting too much of us. There would be these lovely clips of us as youthful creatures and then we would appear as we are now, bald and fat. I for one actually thought that a quick two-minute sketch for the millennium show might affect our chances of a proper reunion show for our thirtieth anniversary the following year. That shows how little I know!'

In fact, in a repeat of the situation ten years earlier, a *Monty Python* night in 1999 was not followed by a celebration of *The Goodies* in 2000. Instead Bill guest-starred in *Fun at the Funeral Parlour,* even allowing himself a comic rant about the BBC not repeating the series. 'I was angry about it. I've always been convinced that a repeat series of the best

episodes has been way overdue. It may have had something to do with the fact that we accepted the offer from ITV. But then, Morecambe and Wise went to ITV and the BBC still repeated their old shows. So I don't know. I suppose someone somewhere didn't like the programme and decided not to repeat it and after that every subsequent controller of BBC2 has seemingly had to sign something forbidding them to repeat *The Goodies*! It's part of the job description! They call it "policy". But that policy has to be started by an individual. It's like the *Comic Relief* thing. There was probably a notice on the wall at the BBC saying, "The Goodies are never allowed any more than eighty-five seconds ever and if you break that policy you will be fired from the BBC." And we had to fight for every second, believe me!'

Tim, having campaigned for BBC repeats for many years, is exasperated. 'People think it's *our* fault! People have been coming up to me in the street for the last twenty years and moaning, "Why won't you let them repeat *The Goodies*?" It's never been anything to do with us. All three of us have always wanted the show repeated, it just never happened.'

But 2000 did have some bright spots. In April, Channel 4 named the team fifth most successful act in its programme, *Top Ten: Comedy Records*. 'I thought that programme was very good,' remembers Bill. 'We were all interviewed for that one. And I was interviewed for "I Love 1970", which I thought was pretty bad, really. But I was happy to be interviewed for these programmes. I did loads that year. Spangles at Christmas or Flares at Christmas or Something at Christmas! A thing about martial arts. I was everywhere. There was this strange fascination with the 1970s and it was obviously bringing good viewing figures, because the programmes were continually being made. I had to be careful at the time because I was doing lots of wildlife shows for BBC2, but Jane Root, in charge at the time, was an inveterate non-*Goodies* fan and had been quoted as saying, "*Goodies* repeats over my dead body!" sort of thing!

'With the greatest respect to her, that simply shouldn't matter. She wasn't running the channel for her benefit. She shouldn't make judgements of what is good or not good in her opinion. If the public wanted to see the show they should have been allowed to see it. But, you know, good, bad or indifferent. It doesn't matter how you perceive *The Goodies*. Whatever you thought of the programme, in terms of that 1970s nostalgia we were a valuable social benchmark for what the decade was all about. We did cover all the fashions of the seventies, so the Goodies' take on punk, or the Goodies' take on *Jaws* or whatever would have had relevance to a documentary about life in the 1970s. But we didn't get anything on television. Not even in a "Can You Ever Believe This Was Considered Funny?" theme night!'

But on 23 May 2000, the team was reunited live on stage at the National Film Theatre for a sell-out interview. 'We assumed after the eighties and nineties that no showings of *The Goodies* meant that the series would be completely forgotten,' laments Tim. 'Suddenly, an invitation to host a *Goodies* evening at the NFT arrived. We thought that a small gathering would be there, but to our surprise and delight the theatre was overflowing. It was a special occasion and great to see members of *The League of Gentlemen* in the audience.'

The standing ovation the team received that night was proof positive that here was a show worth resurrecting.

Finally, Network did. 'We are very much indebted to Tim Beddows from Network,' says Tim. 'In spite of being given a difficult time by the BBC he ploughed ahead in the belief that there was a market for *Goodies* DVDs, and how right he was. But he didn't just bung them on, he had them remastered, so the finished product is infinitely superior to the originals.' Two collections, *The Goodies … At Last* and *The Goodies … At Last A Second Helping,* were international bestsellers and promoted another wave of interest in the team. The Goodies obliged with personal appearances to promote the discs. Interest continued with the trio interviewed for *Comedy Connections*: 'The Goodies' and a two-part Radio 2 documentary *No Fixed Abode, Crickelwood.* Tim and Graeme had been very active in the *Goodies* fan club based in Australia. They had even travelled

Down Under to conventions. And even when *The Goodies* wasn't on the agenda, the stars of the show couldn't escape from all things ecky thump and giant beanstalks. 'A few years ago I went to Australia,' says Bill. 'Actually I was going over there to promote wildlife issues and conservation and the like. As is the norm for those sort of things, I was booked on loads of radio and television programmes to talk about wildlife. And, of course, all these interviewers wanted to know about was *The Goodies*. The show has never been away as far as the Australians are concerned. It seems to be going out all the time over there. There's no escape. I could have watched *The Goodies* any hour of the day if I had had the urge to do so!'

In March 2005, director John Pinder presented them as the headline act at Sydney's Big Laugh Comedy Festival. 'We were invited at the end of 2004 to do a show at the Riverside Theatre,' says Tim. 'Although we knew, thanks to the wonderful Goodies' fan site 'Goodies Rule', we were popular still in Australia, we were dubious that we would attract an audience big enough to justify the production. As it turned out, everything exceeded our expectations. We did shows in Canberra, Sydney, Melbourne and Brisbane, which were all sold out, including two shows in one evening at the Melbourne concert hall. Graeme and I returned in November and, with Bill performing on video, toured all over Australia where we were constantly met with 'Thank you so much for coming'. The audiences were young, enthusiastic and knew a great deal more about the shows than we did. The show was 'The Goodies Still Alive on stage', and featured clips from the shows, re-enactments of programmes like *I'm Sorry I'll Read That Again* and a section on censorship. It also allowed me as president of the Footlights, to re-audition Bill and Graeme."

A return to BBC2 was the next natural step.

Although originally conceived as a Goodies Theme Night, *Return of the Goodies* ended up as a ninety-minute celebration. A 'beginner's guide', according to Tim, the reunion footage was recorded at the London Studios on 23 October. With sets from classic 1970s BBC comedies being discovered as landfill under the millennium dome,

The Goodies were back in 2005. Loud and proud Down Under, their stage shows were a sell-out phenomenon.

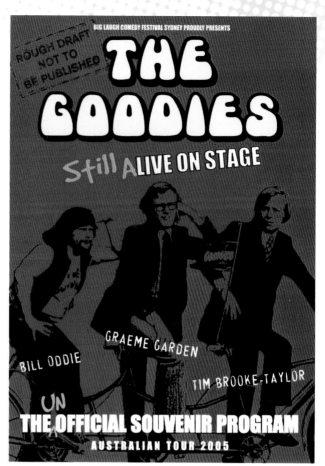

Graeme and Bill break in to their old, abandoned office. Tim is discovered to have spent the previous twenty-five years in the lavatory unaware that he has been trapped in concrete with a studio audience in attendance!

'I wrote the opening and closing,' says Graeme, 'and we all contributed to the rest – a lot of it based on the show we toured in Australia.'

It was recorded at the London Studios, the home of *The Goodies* on ITV. 'It wasn't so strange to go back to the studio,' continues Graeme. 'I'd done many shows there in the interim. It was very weird going into the re-created office set though, with all the props.'

The talking head interviews with guests (Stanley Baxter, Tony Blackburn), directors (Jim Franklin, Bob Spiers), fans (Mark Gatiss, Phill Jupitus) and the Goodies themselves, were interspersed with choice clips and studio reflections by the team. Bill was pleased but indignant: 'It's about bloody time! I thought one of us was going to have to die before the Goodies were back at the BBC!'

While Graeme wryly commented that: 'Even now there's that feeling of we are joined at the hip. I don't mind it, but many people assume that if you've told one of us something we all know it because of some sort of Goody telepathy. People assume we all live in the same house in Cricklewood, just sitting around waiting for the call for us to jump on the trandem and get to work!'

And the trandem was brought out of moth-balls for the show although: 'We weren't allowed to ride it,' reflects Graeme, 'because we had no insurance!'

It was a long time in coming for all of the Goodies but the faith in the series was fully justified. When the programme was broadcast on 29 December 2005 it attracted an audience of three-and-a-half million. 'We were a little surprised actually,' says Graeme. 'But it just goes to show that the British viewer still wants to see *The Goodies*. When you think that BBC2's new flag-ship comedy series, *The Thick of It*, got around a million viewers it is clear that there is life in *The Goodies* yet.' "We're never not wanted to do more episodes" says Tim "although I've

got the feeling we're probably past it now! We always played our own ages whenever the show was made, so that's not really a problem. There's a real sense of frustration when a period of time throws up topics we would dearly like to have a go at. The Falklands War would have been perfect. The Gulf wars. Europe. All that sort of stuff. I would still love to be an active Goody.' Although Bill believes 'we'd do it even better now than we did then, to be honest', he continues that: 'I hope the success of the show [*Return of the Goodies*] doesn't mean they want us to do any more. As far as a reunion is concerned that was it I'm afraid. Although I'm more than happy if they want to repeat the old ones.' Indeed, on 4 March 2006, BBC2 repeated the 'Winter Olympics'. It was the first BBC repeat in twenty years and heralds a new 'policy' that *The Goodies* will be repeated to reflect a current news story in the future.

In the meantime, Tim and Graeme took a live show, 'The Goodies Still Rule OK', to the Edinburgh Festival in August 2006, with a cyber-Bill contributing to the sketches and memories. It was *the* hot ticket of the season.

Tim, Graeme and Bill have been Goodies for thirty-five years: 'Christ, that's over half of my life!' confirms Bill.

But for Tim it's a legacy to be suitably proud of. 'Interviewers always ask, "Would you be annoyed if I mentioned the Goodies?"' he says. 'Frankly, I'd be rather cross if people didn't mention the Goodies!'

SOME GOODIES GOODIES

DVD

The Goodies...At Last (2003, Network 7952171)
The Goodies...At Last A Second Helping (2005, Network 7952172)

CD

The Complete A Poke in the Eye with a Sharp Stick (1991,
Castle/Essential! Records ACSCD 020)
Yum Yum! The Very Best of The Goodies (1997, Music Club MCCD 294)
Funky Gibbon – The Best of the Goodies (2000, Castle Pie PIESD 243)
Laughing Stock – The Best of Classic British Comedy (2002, Sanctuary
Records CMDDD 403)

WEBSITE

www.goodiesruleok.com